A Light on the Path

With you is the fountain of life,
and by your light we are enlightened.
Psalm 36:9

A Light on the Path

An Exploration of Integrity
through the Psalms

MARTIN ISRAEL

Darton, Longman and Todd
London

First published in 1990 by
Darton, Longman and Todd Ltd
89 Lillie Road, London SW6 1UD

British Library Cataloguing in Publication Data
Israel, Martin
  A Light on the path.
  1. Bible. O.T. Psalms – Devotional works
  I. Title
  242.5

ISBN 0–232–51900–5

Phototypeset by Input Typesetting Ltd, London SW19 8DR
Printed and bound in Great Britain by
Courier International Ltd, Tiptree, Essex

To Kathleen
for her original suggestion
to write this book

Contents

Acknowledgement

The extracts from the psalms, and the other scriptural quotations, are taken from the Revised English Bible © 1989 by permission of Oxford and Cambridge University Presses.

1

The Value of the Psalms

The psalms are the religious poetry of Israel. The name is derived from the Greek *psalterion*, which was a string instrument used for accompanying them when they were sung. Amongst their number are hymns of praise, songs of deliverance, and solemn entreaties. Some of them are personal complaints and others national prayers and confessions for past misdemeanours. They mirror the mood of the writer, and by extension speak closely to our condition also. The outer world has changed beyond recognition since the days of the Psalmist (some 2,500 to 3,000 years ago for the majority of the 150 psalms), but human nature remains distressingly immature even though the mind has virtually exploded in scientific brilliance. The writers of the Bible would rub their eyes if they could witness our present civilization, but then they would shake their heads when they saw humans walking around as spiritually uncomprehending as their own brethren.

The psalms are traditionally attributed to King David himself, but only seventy-three are inscribed directly to him. Twelve are inscribed to Asaph, eleven to the sons of Korah, and one each to Heman, Ethan, Moses and Solomon. The sons of Korah, mentioned in 1 Chronicles 9:19, were guards of the thresholds of the Temple, while Asaph, Heman and Ethan (or Jeduthun) were cantors appointed by David for service in the Temple (1 Chron. 25:1–7). Asaph is also mentioned in 1 Chronicles 16 as being entrusted with David's song of praise which follows (verses 8–36). Heman and Ethan were also sages of the east whose wisdom was surpassed by that of Solomon (1 Kings 4:31). In fact we are unsure of the authorship of the psalms; it is possible that the original purpose of the various inscriptions was not so much to name the actual author as to establish some kind of relationship between the psalm and the person named. The psalms for the sons of Korah were part of the repertoire of this family of cantors, just as the numerous psalms 'for the choirmaster' were performed under his direction. As the excellent introduction to the authorship and dates of the psalms in the Standard Edition of the Jerusalem Bible goes on to explain, the same is probably true of collections under the names of Asaph and David. Nevertheless we should not disregard the ancient and valuable information embodied in the inscriptions. While it may well be that the collections of Asaph and the sons of Korah were composed by poets attached to the Temple, there may also be some direct connection between the Davidic collection and the king himself. He is celebrated in the pages of the Bible for his musical talent (1 Sam. 16:16–18), his gifts as a poet (2 Sam. 1:19–27; 3:33–34) and his love of liturgy (2 Sam. 6:5; 15–16), and so it would be surprising if the psalter did not contain some of his work.

Historically some of the psalms obviously mirror the period of return of the Jews from Babylonian exile. The Psalms of the Kingship of God, discussed on pages 118–24, re-echo many of the earlier psalms and also the theology of the second part of the Book of Isaiah (beginning at chapter 40), but it is doubtful whether many psalms date from the Maccabaean period. It is good to think back on David, who 'was the singer of Israel's psalms' (2 Sam. 23.1): his life with its moral frailty, humility and courage are the deeper inspiration of the whole collection. We need his faith even today.

The psalms have afforded consolation to generations of humans in misery and sickness. They have also been on the lips of exultant throngs as victory odes or part of the liturgy of great festivals. Originally confined to Jewish worship, they were transported intact by the Christian Church, and have been the staple of worship for religious communities down the ages. It is moving to attend the offices of such a community, and also instructive to note the discipline of devotion to the words of many centuries past still re-echoing in the spirituality of the present. At each office a sequence of psalms is sung; as one listens, so one is carried back in time to the earliest groups chanting in glorious plainsong. The continuity of witness is very impressive, as is the familiar doxology: 'Glory be to the Father, and to the Son, and to the Holy Spirit; as it was in the beginning, is now, and ever shall be, world without end'. The constant chanting of the psalm brings us to the foundation of stability in God even when we are outwardly buffeted by the distractions of the world. And so the doxology is fulfilled as we live our earthly lives here now.

A psalm or two are usually sung in the course of general church worship, and we gradually become familiar with those that especially appeal to us. It would be ingenuous to believe that all the psalms are of equal spiritual value; some are so filled with cursing or the desire for violent revenge that they are best reserved for private reading. The Psalmist, like ourselves, has his 'off-days', and it is good to be reminded of the inequality of his production when we too feel very angry, depressed, or frankly destructive. As he brought his bad mood to God, so may we also bring our own. God accepts us as we are, and realizing this, a burden is lifted from us and we may then proceed to the work in hand with relief – and perhaps a little humour also. Our problems, like those of Job, pale into insignificance when we consider the glory of creation and revel in the privilege of having been born human. But then we are here to play our part in the world's development to spiritual excellence.

It is uncanny how a particular psalm, or perhaps only a verse or a simple phrase, seems to 'turn up' when we are in special need. Such a piece may be prayed, just as we pray the Lord's Prayer when we are really attentive and do not merely 'rattle it off' as part of daily worship. This way of prayer is one of meditating deeply on the words, putting oneself in the position of attention to God, and being quite still. As we enter the depth of the passage, so does God enter more fully into our own depth, which is the soul, or true self. It is here that our real identity is known, and from it we may speak with personal integrity to God and to our neighbour also.

There is a strong link between the psalms and the New Testament. The great, and very terrible, Psalm 110 is a Messianic forecast of the advent of Christ, as we read in Hebrews 5:5–6. The violence portrayed at the end of the psalm was to be fulfilled in the sufferings of Jesus himself rather than the fierce anger visited by God on the world. The much more reassuring Psalm 91 was actually quoted by the devil when Jesus was tempted in the wilderness (Matt. 4:6). Jesus himself quotes from Psalm 110, which he assumes to be written by David, to point to a deeper origin of the unexpected Messiah than that predicted by the theologians (Mark 12:35–37). But the greatest quotations come when Jesus hangs suspended from the cross: 'My God, my God, why have you forsaken me?' (Mark 15:34) and, 'Father, into your hands I commit my spirit' (Luke 23:46). The psalm texts are 22:1 and 31:5 respectively.

This book has been written primarily for those who know little about the psalms. I hope that my own enthusiasm for them may be transmitted to the enquiring reader, so that he or she may be stimulated to explore this treasury of human spiritual experience. I have purposely quoted many passages so as to whet the appetite of the seeker, and here I am grateful for the translation in the Revised English Bible. While the modern translations lack the memorable poetry of the Authorized Version, they are more accurate and also decidedly more intelligible. The scheme of development that I have chosen in the chapter headings is symbolic of our origin in God and our final return to the Source. And so we descend from God's glory to the very different human situation and our way of life. Then come the negative experiences of spiritual dereliction, fear and trouble, and how the Psalmist has also met them and coped with their terrors. The reward of suffering is the natural outcome of this dark encounter, and we learn the necessity for penitence in respect of what harm we have done to others and our own bodies by thoughtless, selfish living. Then we may enter the daylight once more and enjoy the time and the season of our life in the place where we find ourselves. And so we return to God, but this time as experienced people, able to accept his love in praise and joyful living. His glory has been intensified by our own conscious participation in it. One can hardly avoid comparisons with Christ's incarnation, ministry, suffering, death, resurrection and final ascension to his seat of equality with the Father. But he is even greater than before he came down to earth, for, in human form, he has triumphed over the prince of this world whom we call the devil, however we may understand this term. Furthermore he brings our humanity with him to the Godhead as a promise of the world's eventual deification.

A considerable number of psalms have been included. They are among my favourites, and also speak to a variety of human situations. May they enter into the lives of those who read this book!

2

The Glory of God

The vast cosmic process challenges and transcends human power; the mind falters before its very magnitude. Modern cosmologists speak of an enormous explosion some 15,000 million years ago that was the beginning of the universe. This is an expanse containing innumerable galaxies in which our own solar system is a ludicrously tiny part. And yet God chose to establish the means by which the human could evolve, with his amazing mental capacity and creative potentiality, in a single planet within that solar system.

The human may be frail in his bodily power, but his mind can range at will over such enormous domains that the universe itself is within the bounds of his imagination. Indeed, the human spirit can transcend even the limits of the inexpressibly vast universe and enter into the heart of the mystery through mystical union with the Creator whom we call God. And so we are shown that the material world is not the end, but rather an outer form of a reality so infinite that to enter into it is the meaning of eternal life. What the scientist is obliged to quit in sheer ignorance is the realm of divine knowledge; its standard of assessment is spiritual awareness and growth in rather the same way that the various finite systems of quantity, such as time, size or heat, have within them their own units of measurement.

The Psalmist, like the writer of the Genesis narrative, knew intuitively of a creative power far beyond human delineation, let alone calculation. The mystic, by contrast, knows of the indwelling nature of that power both in the human soul and in the cosmic process, of which the climactic events of our own earth are a very small sample. Direct mystical experience

6

is not stressed, or even advocated, in the orthodox stream of any of the three great monotheistic religions (Judaism, Christianity and Islam), where God's triumphant transcendence is celebrated. Nevertheless the human soul moves according to the work of God's Spirit into deeper realms of inner knowledge, where the divine presence is even clearer than in any outer realm of space and time. Our intelligence may point to an infinite Creator of the finite universe, but our true self, or soul, knows of a direct relationship of pure love whereby both that universe and our own being are filled with energy and animated with life.

It is the God of immediate spiritual experience that the Bible expounds, and the psalms are immortal testimonies of the experience of the divine/human relationship that is the foundation of all meaningful existence. This relationship flows out of the hearts of the poets of Israel as psalms that celebrate the seasons of triumph and bewail the frequent periods of personal pain and national distress.

The glorious Psalm 19 celebrates the creative power of God, maker of the cosmos (the universe and the encompassing intermediate dimension in which the souls of the deceased work in fellowship with the vast angelic hosts) and author of the Law that was given to Moses on Mount Sinai at the time of the exodus of the Israelites from Egypt:

> The heavens tell out the glory of God,
> heaven's vault makes known his handiwork.

The entire celestial company praise God silently by their very presence day by day and night by night, while the glory of the sun shines forth:

> In the heavens an abode is fixed for the sun,
> which comes out like a bridegroom from the bridal
> chamber,
> rejoicing like a strong man to run his course.

Then the writer moves from the constructive excellence of the universe to an exultation in the Law:

The law of the Lord is perfect and revives the soul.
The Lord's instruction never fails;
it makes the simple wise,
The precepts of the Lord are right
and give joy to the heart.
The commandment of the Lord is pure
and gives light to the eyes.

The Lord's judgements are true and greatly to be desired, for they act as a moral warning, while obedience brings a great reward. Then follows a request that the Lord may cleanse the Psalmist from any hidden fault or unwitting sins, that he may also protect him from wilful sins lest they prevail. Only thus can a person remain blameless and innocent of any grave offence. In all this we see the two faces of God's creative act: the cosmos in its terrifying glory and the Law whereby that cosmos is governed and the human creature groomed for his work of dominion over the natural order, thus acting as an assistant to the Creator. In the ancient East the sun was a symbol of justice, and so it holds together the creative power of God and the law whereby every action is governed.

St Paul attacked the Law quite severely in his letters to the Galatians and the Romans. This was not because he disagreed with its moral precepts, which are, after all, the foundation of civilized living. But the Law simply lays down rules without giving the individual the power to obey them. In fact, if he has an especially well-developed power of will and actually succeeds in following the Law's demands, he is liable to self-inflation like the Pharisee in the famous parable of Luke 18:9–14. The end is a loveless perfection of detail with a heart of stone. It is only when the creative power of God enters the life of the spiritual aspirant that love informs his actions. Then only can the Law be obeyed as a natural inclination of the palpitating heart, and the person rises in stature as an essential worker with God in the raising up of the universe from death to immortality. The whole scheme of human life is one of entering more fully into the life of God, so that the highly gifted creature may approximate ever more fully the divine stature as revealed in Jesus, who had the power and authority to raise the very dead back to earthly life.

The psalm ends with the famous supplication:

> May the words of my mouth and the thoughts of my
>   mind
> be acceptable to you,
> Lord, my rock and my redeemer!

These words and thoughts are our own contribution to God's ceaseless creation. If they are ill chosen they can have a destructive power at variance with the divine will. In other words, if we are fellow workers with Jesus in the healing of the world, our attitudes must approach his: there must be no selfishness or personal ambition. This high spiritual state is unattainable by the unaided human will, therefore we have to learn the secret of stillness so as to allow the divine alchemy time to transmute our baser emotions and selfish attitudes into a radiant awareness. Then only can we hear the inner voice of God and do the works that are required.

It is evident that the naked will has a perverse trend no matter how fine our motives may be; St Paul laments our divided consciousness only too well in Romans 7:13–21. Nevertheless our frail human will is capable of one essential action without which God himself cannot help us, the stilling of the mind in full awareness of the present moment. This was what Mary chose in the story of Jesus' visit to her and her sister Martha's home (Luke 10:38–42), while Martha was concerned about so many things and becoming more and more emotionally fraught as a result. Once we, like Mary, are consciously open to God, he will cease to knock at the door of the soul because he is bade welcome. He will enter the inner room with pleasure and sit down to dine with us at our frugal repast. At once it will become a heavenly banquet. Our thoughts and words are always acceptable to God once they are confided in calm awareness. Then at last he is able to redeem us from the prison of earthly preoccupations, so that we may grow to adult stature, less concerned with worldly things as ends in themselves and more devoted to spreading love in whatever company we may find ourselves, rather like Jesus at the parties of the less acceptable members of his own society. Thus do we also play our part in God's continuous creative activity.

Psalm 29 celebrates God's mighty power even more realistically. The angels themselves are told to ascribe glory and might to the Lord and to worship him in holy attire. The Lord's voice thunders in glory over the natural scene in the terror of a severe storm:

> The voice of the Lord echoes over the waters;
> the glory of God thunders . . .
> The voice of the Lord breaks the cedar trees,
> the Lord shatters the cedars of Lebanon.
> He makes Lebanon skip like a calf,
> Sirion like a young wild ox.

In this context Sirion is merely the Sidonian name for Lebanon. God's voice causes fire to flame forth, it makes the wilderness writhe in travail; it makes the hinds calve while the forest is stripped bare. Meanwhile everyone glorifies him in the Temple. Finally the psalm ends on a national note with universal overtones:

> The Lord is king above the flood,
> the Lord has taken his royal seat as king for ever.
> The Lord will give strength to his people;
> the Lord will bless his people with peace.

Mention of the flood recalls God's triumphant justice at the time of Noah, a justice that will always be exercised on behalf of his people, initially Israel but eventually the whole world.

This vigorous psalm, like Psalm 19, can be seen on two levels: the creative force of God in nature and his work for the spiritual growth of mankind. In this respect the turbulent elements of nature are analogous to the enemies of Israel, who will be checked once the people are properly directed to the divine service. Once the immeasurable power of God in the natural order is acknowledged, his Law will be written indelibly on our hearts. Strength and peace are the blessings when we work alongside God. This peace is not merely an absence of turmoil. It is, much more, a state of intimate communion with our Creator, from whom nothing needs to be hidden (as in the story of the awakened Adam and Eve who were shamed by their nakedness), and consequently with our fellow creatures also. The end of God's triumph is the reconciliation of his people with him and with one another. The storm, both cosmic and personal, has been stilled by the healing power of the Almighty. But God's work is embodied in the storm also; only in its thunder are our faults revealed, a necessary stage in their slow correction as our personality is made whole. Though God may not be identified with any created entity, his influence permeates all processes especially when we play our part as responsible agents for what is good in the world. Suffering is an inevitable precursor of healing.

A much more intimate understanding of God's glory is to be found in the magnificent Psalm 139, one of the very greatest of the collection. Here the writer meditates on the divine omniscience in relation to his own life, and therefore by extension to all his fellow creatures.

> Lord, you have examined me and you know me.
> You know me at rest and in action;
> you discern my thoughts from afar.

Nothing is hidden from our Creator: he knows the paths we take, not merely physical journeys but also the speculations of our mind, and all our words are already known to him. In another context Jesus tells his disciples that God knows their needs before they can ask him for help (Matt: 6:8). The Psalmist marvels at God's close guardianship; there is clearly a prior knowledge that astounds him. Nor is there any means of escape from the divine presence, for God is everywhere, whether on earth or in the land of the afterlife, and his protection and guidance never fail.

> If I say, 'Surely darkness will steal over me,
> and the day around me turn to night,'

11

> darkness is not too dark for you
> and night is as light as day;
> to you both dark and light are one.

The writer then proceeds to meditate on the mystery of his creation in his mother's womb: his body was no secret to God during the intricate process of foetal development. And then comes the challenging thought:

> Your eyes foresaw my deeds,
> and they are all recorded in your book;
> my life was fashioned
> before it had come into being.

Are our lives indeed predestined? Does God know exactly the means of their termination right at the beginning of conception? Was there indeed a substance of our soul that pre-existed before our present conception and incarnation? Why, we may ask, are some people's lives such a blessing to the world, while the majority fade away into grey anonymity and a few leave a reputation of disgrace behind them? St Paul, in Romans 9:10–21, explores this theme as best he can – on the text 'Jacob I loved and Esau I hated', from Malachi 1:2–3 – but can come to no other conclusion than the inscrutability of the Creator's purposes and the inadmissibility of the creature's holding him to account for his works. I suppose we might thank God for the primary gift of life to which is added the secondary one of participating in human nature. The end, as suggested in 2 Peter 1:4, is to come to share in the very being of God, as revealed in the incarnation of his Son Jesus Christ. But a hard road has to be traversed before that final goal is achieved. Perhaps this is the way in which St Paul's problem will be solved; if so, it will require much working-out of our personal and universal difficulties in a larger milieu far beyond the portals of physical death.

As one grows older, the clearer does it become that a certain way has been fixed, that the apparently chance events were not, after all, fortuitous, that a greater pattern embraced the random occurrences of daily life. One can, of course, like

Jonah, reject the call and go one's own headstrong way, but soon a disaster checks the path, and if one has a special service to give, the humiliation will stand one in good stead as part of one's training. But, at least theoretically, one can remain recalcitrant indefinitely, raging in the hell of one's own making both in this life and the next. We can only hope that eventually the person will, like the Prodigal Son, come to himself (the modern translations read 'come to his senses', which is more explicit but lacks the concept of the soul's deeper integrity), throw himself at God's mercy, receive absolution, and start the proper life that was for so long evaded. One remembers Shakespeare's lines in *Julius Caesar*:

> There is a tide in the affairs of men,
> Which, taken at the flood, leads on to fortune;
> Omitted, all the voyage of their life
> Is bound in shallows and in miseries.

This seems to be the point of reconciliation between free will and predestination, both of which are true in their own compass. It seems quite possible that the Creator does not know the outcome of any person's life in advance; the universe evolves according to its own inherent life that has been given by God, and natural catastrophes are part of the working-out of its destiny. Nevertheless the Creator is in overall charge, and we may hope that there are contingency plans for an unforeseen emergency. 'All things work together for good for those who love God', as St Paul says in Romans 8:28, and we must hope that their good fortune will bring succour to the remainder of creation also. This seems to be the greater meaning of Christ's incarnation.

The Psalmist marvels at God's creativity; his thoughts are infinite and beyond all human reckoning. After a passage of hatred against all God's adversaries, there is a final plea for the divine assistance in the course of the writer's life:

> Examine me, God, and know my mind,
> test me, and understand my anxious thoughts.

Watch lest I follow any path that grieves you;
lead me in the everlasting way.

This thought brings us close to the end of Psalm 19. It stresses the primacy of prayer in our approach to the Creator; instead of constant shallow thought there is an aware, receptive silence in which we can hear and respond.

Let us end on a more extrovert celebration of God's glory. The thoroughly delightful Psalm 104 describes the wonder of creation itself. It brings us to the perennial freshness of the countryside and the joy in being able to share in the life of our fellow creatures in the vegetable and animal kingdoms. Since the sequence follows the creation narrative of Genesis 1, there is first a description of the heavens with God himself above them:

Bless the Lord, my soul.
Lord my God, you are very great,
clothed in majesty and splendour,
and enfolded in a robe of light.

The heavens are spread out like a tent, while God takes the clouds as a chariot, and rides on the wings of the wind. The earth is fixed on its foundation in close relation with its seas and rivers, which, since the great flood of Noah's time, are strictly bounded lest they cover the earth again. Then follows a more intimate picture of the country:

You make springs break out in the wadis,
so that water from them flows between the hills.
The wild beasts all drink from them,
the wild donkeys quench their thirst;
the birds of the air nest on their banks
and sing among the foliage.

God's providence ensures that the earth is enriched, while the vegetation grows for human needs and animal survival:

You make grass grow for the cattle
and plants for the use of mortals,
producing grain from the earth,
food to sustain their strength,
wine to gladden the hearts of the people,
and oil to make their faces shine.

In the riches of trees live the various birds, while the high
hills are a haunt of the mountain goat, and crags a cover for
the rock-badger. An especially magical passage describes the
transitions of the sun and moon and the times of the day:

You bring darkness, and it is night,
when all the beasts of the forest go prowling;
the young lions roar for prey,
seeking their food from God;
when the sun rises, they slink away
and seek rest in their lairs.
Man goes out to his work
and his labours until evening.

The Psalmist marvels at God's prodigality: by his wisdom he
had made them all, and the earth is full of his creatures. The
sea is vast, and is inhabited by a numerous progeny, living
creatures of all sizes and also ships sailing to and fro. Mention
is made too of Leviathan, traditionally a monster of primeval
chaos, but in this context, as in Job 41, a description of the
whale:

All of them look to you in hope
to give them their food when it is due.
What you give them they gather up;
when you open your hand, they eat their fill of good
    things.
When you hide your face, they are dismayed.
When you take away their spirit, they die
and return to the dust from which they came.
When you send forth your spirit, they are created;
and you give new life to the earth.

> May the glory of the Lord stand for ever,
> and may the Lord rejoice in his works!

With this delicious thought we may take leave of this psalm, finding as much happiness in the creation as did the writer himself, who vowed to sing to the Lord as long as he lived, to sing psalms all his life long, praying that his meditation might be acceptable to God.

> Praise the Lord, my soul.
> Praise the Lord.

The child-like delight of this psalm puts its range far beyond earthly considerations without in the least impugning their immediate importance. If only we could take a fresh delight in the scene around us, we would live consciously in the present moment, which is also the heaven of eternity. The glory of God would never leave our view even when we were suffering grievously as part of our growth into proficiency from childishness to adult responsibility.

3

The Human Condition

The Psalmist enjoys a very personal relationship with God. His moods alternate between extravagant praise and downcast irritation, between high aspiration and dark despair, between universal charity and sharp cursing of enemies. Some of these moods are quite embarrassing to the aspiring Christian, and provide grist to the mill of a sophisticated generation that finds religious observance generally distasteful because of the demands it makes on its personal integrity. If the declarations of the Psalmist are as banal as this, we can well do without them and follow some more contemporary spirituality, so would run the argument. But in the end we are forced back upon ourselves, and the finest intentions tend to founder in a shallow sea of selfishness, jealousy and petty dishonesty, to say nothing of various sexual misdemeanours. In a wiser moment we may be thrown back upon the ageless wisdom of the psalms, and see ourselves disconcertingly portrayed in more than one of its vignettes. Human creativity seems to have no end, but human nature remains distressingly immature; suffering well digested seems an inevitable precursor of the growing process, and the Bible is a useful commentary in the lives of many of its protagonists. The psalms themselves are essentially anonymous, but the characters it delineates can usually be matched by what we feel inside ourself.

The longest of them all is Psalm 119. As the admirable footnote in the Standard Edition of the Jerusalem Bible tells us, the psalm is one of the most remarkable monuments of Israelite devotion to the divine revelation. The Law or one of its corresponding terms, like decree, precept, statute, promise, commandment, word, judgement or way, is found in nearly every one of the 176 verses. But more than simply a lengthy eulogy on the Law, it is also an allegory of the soul's travail in search of God, whose ways are enshrined in the Law. There is first of all a passage of praise to God for his Law and a pledge to conform to it (the psalm is conveniently read in sequences of sixteen verses):

> How may a young man lead a clean life?
> By holding to your words.
> With all my heart I seek you;
> do not let me stray from your commandments.

Then comes the descent into the world of affairs with all its temptations to conform to its baser counsels; the Psalmist invokes the divine help in his moments of isolation, and the Law is his constant consolation. There follows a prayer for God's help that he may understand the Law better:

> Teach me, Lord, the way of your statutes,
> and in keeping them I shall find my reward.
> Give me the insight to obey your law
> and keep it wholeheartedly.

It would seem that the supplication has been heard, for the writer shows a much more resolute frame of mind, but soon he is confronted once again with human hostility, and calls frantically on the name of the Lord for help. As he battles with everyday events, so the fruit of suffering becomes more apparent. The outcome of this encounter is a greater wisdom that in turn facilitates an understanding of the Law.

> You are good, and what you do is good;
> teach me your statutes.
> I follow your precepts wholeheartedly . . .
> How good it is for me to have been chastened,
> so that I might be schooled in your statutes!
> The law you have ordained means more to me
> than a fortune in gold and silver.

Indeed, it is the experience of suffering that makes the law shine more radiantly inasmuch as travail cuts down to size all previously valued commodities:

> Let your love comfort me,
> as you have promised me, your servant,
> Extend your compassion to me, that I may live,
> for your law is my delight.

But the pain does not diminish:

> Though I shrivel like a wineskin in the smoke,
> I do not forget your statutes.
> How long must I, your servant, wait?
> When will you execute judgement on my persecutors?

Once again the divine assistance comes just in time to save him:

> Had your law not been my delight,
> I should have perished in my distress;
> never shall I forget your precepts,
> for through them you have given me life.

But the menace of the wicked ones still lies in wait to attack him; God alone is his strength:

> I see all things have an end,
> but your commandment has no limit.

The wisdom already known now grows in authority, for God is the source of this quality which is beyond all price:

> Your word is a lamp to my feet,
> a light on my path;
> I have bound myself by oath and solemn vow
> to keep your just decrees . . .
> Every day I take my life in my hands,
> yet I never forget your law.

And so the psalm moves on to its slow close: continual suffering, prayer to God, strength given, and the path of life resolutely trodden. The Psalmist is outraged at the arrogance with which the world treats God and his supreme revelation, the Law. Nevertheless he is aware how far from God he himself remains despite his protestations of loyalty:

> In your dealings with me, Lord, show your love
> and teach me your statutes.
> I am your servant; give me insight
> to understand your instruction.

In his work for God and his righteousness he is continually assailed by the foe:

> I am speechless with indignation
> at my enemies' neglect of your words.
> Your promise has been well tested,
> and I love it, Lord.
> I may be despised and of little account,
> but I do not forget your precepts.

And so the Psalmist continues to pray faithfully to God, though constantly pursued by malicious enemies, who in fact are the unenlightened people of the world whose god is their own senses. To gratify them is their life's end.

> Seven times each day I praise you for the justice of your
> decrees.

The final verse is especially moving:

> I have strayed like a lost sheep;
> come, search for your servant,
> for I have not forgotten your commandments.

This is the essential human condition, striving for an excellence that is deeply implanted within the soul and being repeatedly drawn away from the great quest by diverting, though essentially trivial, mundane considerations. Nevertheless, like the constantly apostasizing people of Israel, we are drawn back to the work by prophets without and the divine spark within; the former relight the latter when it is all but extinguished by the crowd pressing in on it.

The lovely Psalm 42–43 (despite their separate numbers they are really one continuous entreaty to God) expresses the lament of a devout Jew, a Levite, who finds himself in exile from Jerusalem and its Temple, the focus of true worship to the one God.

> As a hind longs for the running streams,
> so I long for you, my God.
> I thirst for God, the living God;
> when shall I come to appear in his presence?

He cries bitter tears when the foreigners ask where his God is. He remembers in deep distress the glorious march to the Temple in the past:

> How deep I am sunk in misery, groaning in my distress!
> I shall wait for God; I shall yet praise him,
> my deliverer, my God.

The pain of past memories contrasting with the humiliation and loneliness of the present punctuate the progress of the psalm:

> Deep calls to deep in the roar of your cataracts,
> and all your waves, all your breakers, sweep over me.

At the same time, however, there is an even deeper hope:

> By day the Lord grants his unfailing love;
> at night his praise is upon my lips,
> a prayer to the God of my life.

Rather like Psalm 119, but in much smaller compass and with a stark tragedy to relate, the course of this psalm contrasts the

21

divine help and the pain of the present time. But there is strength to wait in patience for God's deliverance. In the Psalm 43 portion it would seem that the writer has had to contend with evil people in addition to being exiled from his home, somewhat reminiscent of the suffering Christ, but once again there is a deeper trust in God's future providence.

While alive in the flesh we are all necessarily exiles from the kingdom of God, which, as Wordsworth put it in his 'Ode on Intimations of Immortality' in *Recollections of Early Childhood,* is our true home. Just as the Israelites learned many valuable lessons in patience, humility and diligence during their Babylonian exile, so that they could return home as fully-fledged Jews ready to receive the teaching of Ezra, so we too learn similar lessons on the hard path of life. Bereavement, of which exile is a special category, teaches us to lay no great stress on worldly things, even human relationships if used to allay loneliness, but to put our trust in God alone, who is the supreme imperishable amid a chaos of change and destruction. In the psalm the Temple is the sacrament of the divine presence, but that too had to be destroyed before a new one could be built by the returning exiles under the leadership of Zerubbabel. The chastened community worshipped more devoutly than in the past, because they had been deprived of their overall power and depended entirely on the kindness of the ruling countries and the love of God. But even the second Temple was eventually destroyed in AD 70, and has never been replaced. The vicissitudes of life bring us home, from where we originally set out but now for the first time really knowing its contours, as T. S. Eliot reflected at the end of *Little Gidding.* That home is heaven, but of a very different nature from the traditional abode portrayed in fiction. It is full of the sweat and hard work of the multitudes working together for the healing of creation and the coming again of the Lord: 'Heaven and earth will pass away, but my words will never pass away' (Mark 13:31).

Fortunately, however, our lives are not only a continual saga of pain and exile. There is also a joyful side, full of wonder and delight. So runs the short, lovely Psalm 8. Here, in contrast with Psalm 19, the glory of God in creation is juxtaposed with human frailty, seen in its most moving form, in the person of a little child:

> Your majesty is praised as high as the heavens,
> from the mouths of babes and infants at the breast.

When the Psalmist contemplates the immensity of the heavenly firmament, he marvels equally at the significance the Creator has placed in his human creation. He is a frail mortal, and yet he has been made little less than a god, crowned, at least potentially, with glory and honour. All the other created forms of our world, animal, plant and mineral, are under human control. In the time of the Bible this subjection of the earth to human domination was neutral, if not always benign, but now its malignant propensity is too well-known to demand special comment; a century that has witnessed wholesale genocide is only now reacting sharply to the destruction of the ecological systems upon which we all depend for our sustenance.

> When I look up at your heavens, the work of your
>   fingers,
> at the moon and the stars you have set in place,
> what is a frail mortal, that you should be mindful of
>   him,
> a human being, that you should take notice of him?

This too is the human condition: we have been made little less than a god, which in this context means a creature with a will sufficiently free to make conscious moral choices. In the Creation allegory Adam and Eve appropriated the way of moral choice, figuratively partaking of the fruit of the tree of the knowledge of good and evil, without prior reference to the Creator God. We cannot in fact know true moral judgement apart from divine guidance; once we take matters into our own hands without reference to a higher source, we make ourselves gods and the final results are always unfortunate. We begin to judge and condemn other people when viewed against the backcloth of our own prejudices. When we return to the second simplicity of childhood, we are open in innocence to the call of the present moment, and the Creator can work with us as responsible partners in the never-ending work of maintaining what is and creating what is to be. We add our unique contribution under the guidance of the Holy Spirit.

The fine series of psalms from 120 to 134 are entitled collectively Songs of the Ascents. They are all, with the exception of Psalm 132, short, and were sung by pilgrims on the way to Jerusalem. This could form a magnificent theme for meditation: a company of pilgrims chanting these lovely psalms, each replete with fiery emotion tempered with the wisdom of experience and the reticence of past humiliation, as they march through waterless valleys to the great city, as Psalm 84, another song of pilgrimage, so beautifully puts it. Each psalm speaks to the human condition because it relates eternal truths of that condition, as does all authentic spiritual writing.

One of the favourites of the series is Psalm 121:

> If I lift up my eyes to the hills,
> where shall I find help?
> My help comes only from the Lord,
> maker of heaven and earth.

The psalm confesses our human impotence apart from the divine assistance. If we play our part he will not let us make a false movement, for he is our guardian and he never falls asleep, unlike even the most trustworthy human protection. Neither the sun nor the moon can assail us against the loving care of God, our supreme guardian as we come and go, now and for ever more. In this life, nevertheless, we shall not escape danger and trouble as common experience shows us, but we need not be overwhelmingly fearful provided we establish a good relationship with God, by the practice of prayer, during the more peaceful periods.

The most significant verse is the first, quoted above. There is no help from even the mightiest potentates or the most impressive occult systems of philosophy. They all fail when they are most urgently required, for they are the works of human hands. As servants they all have their uses, but as guides they soon become idols that prevent the rugged pilgrimage to our own Jerusalem, which is essentially a type of the City of God in the heavens. And yet anyone engaged in wholehearted pilgrimage is in that city even now as he trudges wearily along. It is the love and dedication of his fellows on the way that bring him to a city not built with hands that is eternal. This is where the help comes from as our eyes are lifted up in aspiration.

Psalm 124 celebrates the survival of the Israelites after some battle; it may have been one of the numerous skirmishes recorded in the Books of Samuel or Kings, or even more significantly, the survival of the people after Babylonian captivity, remembering how the inhabitants of the Northern Kingdom of Israel (Samaria) were completely destroyed by the Assyrian hosts. Indeed the amazing story of the survival of the Jews up to our own time is a worthy continuation of this theme:

If the Lord had not been on our side –
let Israel now say –
if the Lord had not been on our side
when our foes attacked,
then they would have swallowed us alive
in the heat of their anger against us.

The Psalmist blesses God for his protective power, that the people escaped like a bird from the fowler's trap. He ends by re-echoing the second verse of Psalm 121, 'My help comes only from the Lord, maker of heaven and earth.' Indeed our own welfare day by day is an act of pure divine grace. When we have the time for a moment's quiet recollection of a single day's activities, we will soon have cause to say, 'But for the grace of God this dreadful thing might have occurred.' Unfortunately we are usually so preoccupied with our current concerns that we forget to thank God for his over-all protection. The chequered history of the Jews made their awareness more acute.

Blessed be the Lord who did not leave us
a prey for their teeth.

This psalm is especially pertinent for those who have survived
some personal ordeal; a major cancer operation is a topical
example, another is the humiliating experience of redun-
dancy. As we grow older, so we begin to recognize the teaching value of adversity bravely confronted. We learn to depend
less on outer circumstances and more on ourselves, who in
turn are inspired by the power of the Holy Spirit. The Israelites lost everything time after time, as did their Jewish
descendants after some terrible persecution, but a mysterious
spirit of hope deep within them kept them on the move when
every logical escape seemed impossible. This again is part of
the human condition; it leads to faith which in turn is fertilized by action.

Another favourite is Psalm 127:

Unless the Lord builds the house,
its builders labour in vain.
Unless the Lord keeps watch over the city,
the watchman stands guard in vain.

The Psalmist goes on to deride those who strive so hard for
the things of this world, for God supplies the need of those
he loves, who, I would add, following the development of
this theme in the Sermon on the Mount (Matt. 6:25–34), is
everything he has caused to be created. Needless to say, all
this admonition does not absolve us from our work in building
edifices, keeping watch at all times lest we fail to receive
Christ when he comes again, at the same time maintaining
the earth in as fine a condition as possible, or seeing to our
day-to-day needs. If we fail to play our part we shall certainly
starve and the world return to primeval chaos. On the other
hand if we work proudly on our own we shall simply construct
a tower of Babel that will disintegrate under the force of our
mutual discord. The ominous events of our own technologically-
advanced century underline this warning.

The psalm ends with an exaltation of human fecundity

with the usual emphasis on sons rather than daughters that runs through the Bible. Already in Genesis 1:22 we read of the blessing given by God to those who are obediently fertile, a blessing to be repeated in verse 28 in respect of the human being. In a more modern context where overcrowding is a major world problem, fertility and fruitfulness can be seen in a more constructive light as a proper husbanding of our own talents. In this way the world can be better managed.

The next psalm (128) exalts family life still further. A fruitful wife and numerous sons around the table are seen as a blessing for those who fear God. To this joy is added prosperity and happiness. The psalm ends with the prayer:

> May the Lord bless you from Zion;
> may you rejoice in the prosperity of Jerusalem
> all the days of your life.
> And may you live to see your children's children!
> Peace be on Israel!

This perspective is typical of the Psalmist; with only a few exceptions his vision is limited to this world. Fertility, prosperity and longevity are the three prizes to which he strains. In themselves they are not to be derided, but their attainment can lead to a smug complacency even when the good of the whole community is borne in mind. There is a nobler, and more realistic, theme to our life: suffering bravely undergone so that we may grow in the eternal knowledge of God. This statement must be made in respect of those who are not fertile, or whose lives, through no apparent fault of their own, do not move in circles of material prosperity or personal health, whether physical or mental. It is most profitable to read Psalms 127 and 128 in the context of Psalm 124: an expression of spontaneous relief and consequent praise to God for the essentials of life that have been granted after some terrible trial. The remarkable history of the Jews throughout the ages amplifies this theme.

A final psalm that illustrates the human condition is one of simple humility. Psalm 131 breathes a childlike trust in the Lord, and as such is good to repeat just before going to sleep at night. There is no pride of heart or haughtiness of eyes, nor does the Psalmist busy himself with great affairs or matters too intricate for his simple brain. He says:

> But I am calm and quiet
> like a weaned child clinging to its mother.
> Israel, hope in the Lord,
> now for evermore.

When Jesus told his disciples, 'Whoever does not accept the kingdom of God like a child will never enter it' (Mark 10:15), he was capturing the meaning of this psalm perfectly. It is important to distinguish between childlikeness and childishness. The childish person is centred on the ego which demands recognition and will not be satisfied until it has won the local conflict. The childlike person, by contrast, is centred on the spirit of the soul where God is known. There is therefore no personal striving but only a complete surrender of the self to God. In such a situation, once the individual has been educated in the school of life, there can be a proper alignment of the divine will and that of the person. In this transaction neither of the two wills is dominant. On the contrary, each works to the fullness of its capacity so that the power of God may come down to earth in the person of the aspirant.

It is right for the young child to be childish, for only thus will its demands be satisfied, but when it grows beyond its parental roof it will be obliged to adapt to many different types of experience if it is to survive. If we all remained at a childish state, we would fight against each other for pre-eminence, and the end would be destruction. Thus St Paul is right: 'When I was a child I spoke like a child, reasoned like a child; but when I grew up I finished with childish things' (1 Cor. 13:11). But we should retain at least something of the primeval childlike wonder and trust of our youth, especially in the midst of a cynical materialistic society. In this way we may bring a knowledge of God to our weary fellows, even when neither we nor they understand what is happening. This is the most telling way of evangelism.

4

The Way of Life

Jesus said, 'Enter by the narrow gate. Wide is the gate and broad the road that leads to destruction, and many enter that way; narrow is the gate and constricted the road that leads to life, and those who find them are few' (Matt. 7:13–14). The way is a common metaphor for the religious path in many traditions, and is mentioned also in Acts 9:2; 18:26, 24:14. It is also, as we have noted on page 18, one of the terms for the Law. The Law was given through Moses to the Israelites that they might live a decent life, but although they often carried out its ritual demands well enough, their hearts were usually far from obeying its moral precepts. Amos and his successors were all as one in condemning them for this higher breach of the Law. In fact only when love rules the heart can the moral law be effortlessly fulfilled, and Christians would see the ministry of Jesus as bringing this love into the hearts of his followers and through them to the world. But the process still continues until every dark thing is brought to light, confessed to God and healed by his love, a love revealed categorically in the passion of his Son. The psalms, all written long before the incarnation, can only grope in this direction, but nevertheless their prescriptions for the good life are very valuable.

Psalm 1 contrasts the ways of the righteous and the sinner very starkly:

> Happy is the one
> who does not take the counsel of the wicked for a
>   guide,
> or follow the paths that sinners tread . . .

> His delight is in the law of the Lord;
> it is his meditation day and night.

He is like a firmly planted tree beside water, its foliage never fades, and he likewise prospers. The wicked, by contrast, are like chaff blown by the wind. The analogy is made more substantial by Jesus at the end of the Sermon on the Mount (Matt. 7:24–27). The psalm ends with the statement of faith in God's protection over the righteous while the way of the wicked is doomed.

In terms of everyday life this view is usually correct; if a person leads a life of moderation and remembers God in his daily work he is much more likely to escape disaster than his heedless, agnostic brother. The life of prayer marshals one's inner resources, and one's relationships are purified as one's health is strengthened. Amongst the prescriptions for the good life, which is also the fulfilled life, are sobriety, chastity and alms-giving. The Law encourages these without detracting from the joy of living. Puritanism on the other hand tends to reject the pleasures of life, which are replaced by a stern, often loveless, type of religion. In due course the repressed drives towards pleasure assert themselves either in being projected on to alien groups, who are then the subject of envy, or else by breaking through the barrier of the person's own unconscious and precipitating wild orgies of profligacy. It is to the credit of Old Testament religion that the earthy part of the personality was not denigrated but rather given its own due in happy family relationships, feasts as well as fasts, and a general rejoicing in the world's fecundity. In this context we remember Psalm 104.

A particularly fine exhortation on this theme is Psalm 34. First there is a general praise to God's presence and his justice:

> I shall bless the Lord at all times;
> his praise will be ever on my lips . . .
> Glorify the Lord with me;
> let us exalt his name together . . .
> Taste and see that the Lord is good . . .

> Princes may suffer want and go hungry,
> but those who seek the Lord lack no good thing.

Then comes the admonition to do good in order to enjoy a long, prosperous life. The main requirements are a still, honest tongue, a turning away from evil and doing good, and living in peace with the world. There follows a typical assertion of God's imminent help to all who do good, while he sets his face against those who do wrong so that their memory is erased from the earth. God is especially close to the cry of the righteous and also to those whose courage is sorely tried and whose spirit is nearly crushed.

> Though the misfortunes of one who is righteous be
>   many,
> the Lord delivers him out of them all.
> He guards every bone of his body, and none of them
>   will be broken.

This verse was fulfilled in John 19:36 in respect of the death of Jesus. The psalm ends on a savage note of punishment for the evildoers while the good person escapes and seeks refuge in God. The particular feature of the psalm that makes it so satisfying is the intimate love of God, closer to us than our dearest friend. In this love we can take our misfortunes in our stride, looking forward confidently to the day of our deliverance and the downfall of our enemies.

This last theme, though real enough to human nature if not to the divine love for all that is created, is the kernel of both Psalms 37 and 73. The first, called 'a mirror of Providence' by Tertullian (according to a footnote in the Jerusalem Bible), compares the fate of the virtuous and the wicked:

> Do not be vexed because of evildoers
> or envy those who do wrong.
> For like the grass they soon wither,
> and like green pasture they fade away.

The verses of this rather long psalm repeat this basic theme with minor variations, but now and then a more practical note is struck:

> Better is the little which the righteous person has
> than all the wealth of the wicked;
> for the power of the wicked will be broken,
> but the Lord upholds the righteous.

One particular portion near the end merits special notice:

> I have seen a wicked man inspiring terror,
> flourishing as a spreading tree in its native soil.
> But one day I passed by and he was gone;
> for all that I searched for him, he was not to be found.

Current history certainly underlines this observation; the events in Eastern Europe have transcended the fondest imagination of the free world. But one has to admit that the sufferings of the oppressed may have to proceed for a long time before the wicked are finally routed. In the same vein the Psalmist finds descendants surviving the honest man, whereas the transgressor and his progeny are all wiped out; again this is a dictum that is generally true, though the modern examples of genocide in our civilized century deserve a respectful caveat.

Psalm 73 is, if anything, even more outspoken on the theme of divine retribution. The writer begins, somewhat ironically it would seem, to praise God for his goodness to the upright and the pure in heart. But then comes the wrench: the all too obvious prosperity of the wicked. While the good man suffers affliction and every morning brings new punishment, it would seem as if the advantage of life does lie with the transgressor. But the Psalmist remains true to God even when he cannot grasp the paradox intellectually. Then suddenly the mystery is explained:

> Indeed you place them on slippery ground
> and drive them headlong into utter ruin!

In a moment they are destroyed,
disasters making an end of them.

It was the embittered mind of the writer that occluded a
deeper understanding, a situation that afflicted Jeremiah likewise in the course of his painful ministry to his ungrateful
fellow countrymen: 'Lord, even if I dispute with you, you
remain in the right; yet I shall plead my case before you.
Why do the wicked prosper and the treacherous all live at
ease?' (Jer. 12:1). Yes indeed the wicked have due punishment to face, but does this help the suffering righteous person?
Poor Jeremiah had to await posthumous recognition by his
fellow Israelites. This brings us to the possibility of personal
survival of death, vague and unsatisfactory in its formulation
at the time the psalms were written:

You guide me by your counsel
and afterwards you will receive me with glory.
Whom have I in heaven but you?
And having you, I desire nothing else on earth.

Psalm 16 indicates how the righteous way may be pursued.
The Psalmist castigates his fellow-countrymen who believe
they can combine the monotheism of the true faith with an
observance of the local cults:

All my delight is in the noble ones,
the godly of the land.
Those who run after other gods find endless trouble;
I shall never offer libations of blood to such gods,
never take their names on my lips.

The praise of the true God is very fine, his gratitude for his
daily providence touching in its sincerity. The psalm is very
suitable for the night, and is sometimes used in the office of
compline:

I shall bless the Lord who has given me counsel:
in the night he imparts wisdom to my inmost being.

33

I have set the Lord before me at all times:
with him at my right hand I cannot be shaken.

Nowadays the danger of religious syncretism is less than that of simply worshipping worldly things as our god. It may require a sharp course of pain to bring us to our senses: material benefits have their limits, but, as Psalm 119 puts it, 'I see that all things have an end, but your commandment has no limit' (verse 96). And so a way of life founded on constant awareness of the divine presence, which is the very practice of prayer, is the impetus by which the proper way of life is followed. There is no guarantee of good fortune, but at least one is aware of a presence of support, strength and also counsel. As in Psalm 73 there is an intimation, little more perhaps than a hope, of personal survival of death as the reward of good living:

Therefore my heart is glad
and my spirit rejoices,
my body too rests unafraid;
for you will not abandon me to Sheol
or suffer your faithful servant to see the pit.

Sheol, like the Greek Hades, was the land the shades, of ghostlike immaterial forms of once living people. It had no personal reality, and the meanest person alive in the flesh was infinitely more fortunate than the erstwhile mighty in the place of the dead. Even as great a prophet as Samuel was to be located there (1 Sam. 28:12–19). A more enlightened view of the afterlife had to await the Maccabaean revolt against the hellenizing policies of Antiochus Epiphanes with the roll of Jewish martyrs that accompanied it (Daniel 12:2 is an important text about the resurrection of the body, while the Book of Wisdom written some hundred years later affirms the immortality of the soul in the third chapter). Nevertheless it must be admitted that even today we have no direct proof of a personal survival, despite the tantalizingly suggestive evidence of near-death experiences and spontaneous apparitions of dead friends who have made the transition. Survival of death, like the existence of God, is something we have to learn through the toil of our own lives; while some people admittedly seem more sensitive to spiritual experience then others, we are all travellers on the way while we are working in our physical body. If we live according to the Law but interpreted by love, we shall know as much as is good for us each moment of our lives on earth. This is the deeper message of Psalm 131.

Psalm 15, which has been called the gentleman's psalm, gives an account of the person who is eligible for divine fellowship. There should be blameless conduct, righteous dealing with others, and truthfulness. There should be no malice lurking in the heart or tale-bearing on the lips. The concern for his fellows should move beyond mere harmlessness to a generosity sufficient to reject any interest on money lent as well as any bribe against the weak and innocent. Such a person shows his scorn for those rejected by God but honours those who fear him. It seems unlikely that a God of love would reject any of his creatures no matter how sinful they were, and it would be preferable to interpret the sentence in terms of the sinful individual rejecting God. The scorn shown should be softened by compassion, lest the righteous person assumes some of the complacent judgementalism of the Pharisee in Luke 18:9–14. This is indeed the limitation of this type of morality, as is seen even more clearly in Psalm 101. Here it is the person in charge who speaks, expounding the qualities of an ideally virtuous householder or ruler, according to how one interprets the words. There is first the customary undertaking to lead a wise and blameless life far removed from any shameful thing. Apostasy is reviled as are crooked thoughts. Then comes a more judgemental part:

> I shall silence those who whisper slanders:
> I cannot endure the proud and the arrogant.
> I shall choose for my companions the faithful in the land;
> my servants will be those whose lives are blameless . . .
> Morning after morning I shall reduce all the wicked to
> silence,
> ridding the Lord's city of all evildoers.

The problem of the evil corrupting the innocent is a perennial one. The downfall of the kingdoms of Israel and Judah started with King Solomon's syncretistic worship of the one true God and the Canaanite deities of his various wives and concubines. After a bedraggled army of survivors returned some 400 years later from Babylonian captivity to repopulate Palestine and rebuild Jerusalem and the Temple, they were chastened and wise enough to heed the injunction of Ezra, some seventy years later, to dissolve all foreign marriages so as to keep a pure, undefiled Judaism. The end of that purity was the person of Jesus, under whose protection it became possible once more to mix freely with all sorts of people. The early Christian community had to learn that God has no favourites, and that gentiles were as acceptable as the Jews who formed the first Christian band. But now the gentiles were no threat to the integrity of the faith in which, as St Paul wrote in Galatians 3:28, there is no such thing as Jew and Greek, slave and freeman, male and female; for all are one person in Christ Jesus. Nevertheless St Paul does warn his Corinthian disciples of the danger of teaming up with unbelievers, and asks what partnership righteousness can have with wickedness. Can light associate with darkness? (2 Cor. 6:14).

One can only comment that it takes a long time for a Christian to assume even a little of the love of his Lord, though in our ravaged century, where all sorts of people who would previously have kept tightly to themselves have been brought very close through adversity (as well as the media of mass-communication), there is a great concern for the welfare of all under-privileged groups as well as the natural environment. We are of necessity all drawing closer together, and provided we hold fast to God in prayer and righteous conduct we need fear the contamination of no one. On the contrary our work, following that of Jesus, is to bring light to the dark areas of the world. In this way Isaiah's glorious prophecy may be fulfilled, 'The people that walked in darkness have seen a great light; on those who lived in a land as dark as death a light has dawned' (Isa. 9:2). Admittedly the incarnation of Christ was the herald of that light, but we ourselves have to complete its illuminating clarity before Christ comes again.

To return to Psalm 101, there can be no working relationship between decency and sin, for the latter would be sure to conquer. But there should be no absolute break in relationship either, lest the wicked faded away in their own perfidy and a part of God's creation lay in ruins. On the other hand the decent folk could easily become complacent and uncompassionate if left to their own devices. Holiness is what we should aspire towards, for in it the presence of God is revealed in all his love. That love brings the decent and the wicked together again in a new relationship, 'For all alike have sinned, and are deprived of the divine glory' (Rom. 3:23).

The Parable of the Publican and the Pharisee in Luke 18:9–14, mentioned already, shows us the true way of life. Though the publican (a venal Jewish tax-gatherer in the pay of the hated Roman occupying army) has nothing to recommend him to mankind, he remains acceptable to God because of his divine creation and his subsequent existence. Once he throws himself without reservation on the divine compassion he is immediately received, and we may assume that he then starts to live a righteous life, for who can know God and remain unregenerate? The virtuous Pharisee, by no means a hypocrite and honest in his religion, is so full of his own excellence that he has no place in it for the wretched publican. In other words his virtue lacks the one needful ingredient of holiness, which is love. St Paul spoke profoundly when he said, 'I may give all I possess to the needy, I may give my body to be burnt, but if I have no love, I gain nothing by it' (1 Cor. 13:3).

It is this love that does not come out in the Psalmist. Like the Law written before him and which he loves so dearly, what he writes is often excellent, but it lacks the driving force that alone will ensure its fulfilment. This is love, which comes from God whose nature is loving. It is much easier to love the Law than to love people; the first is immutable and sound, the second fickle, weak and usually destructive, especially when they are most needed. The passion of Jesus illustrates this theme as does no written commentary: 'I am the way, the truth, and the life; no one comes to the Father except by me' (John 14:6). When we consider these well-known words in the light of what has been written, their truth is obvious without the necessity of any Christian triumphalism.

5

The Dark Hours

In the lives of all spiritual aspirants there are periods when the light of God's presence is so dimmed that all tangible means of support seem to have been removed – if indeed they ever existed as more than a pathetic illusion, conjured up by the mind to evade the challenge of ultimate meaningless with annihilation as its centre. None can escape this experience, any more than Jesus could avoid the pain of his passion and the apparent ignominy of his death. One of the most attractive, indeed lovable, features of the psalms is their strong tendency to get to the heart of the matter, not flinching from even the most direct emotional response at what appears to be God's arbitrary dealings with his creatures, especially the chosen people of Israel. Despair, irritation, anger and growing impatience mark a number of the psalms; their general tenor may make us frown because of their pre-Christian attitudes, but then we have to sit down with our own emotional darkness, and not simply adopt exemplary spiritual poses that serve to separate us from our deeper feelings. These will erupt no matter how carefully they are lulled to sleep in an atmosphere of cosy piety or religious fervour on behalf of a particular cause.

A plea of great urgency is contained in Psalm 142. Here the situation is that of a hunted man who prays in desperation to God for help:

I cry aloud to the Lord;
to the Lord I plead aloud for mercy.

He is in a sad plight, for his enemies are all around him,

seeking to destroy him by sedulously laying snares to trap him.

> I look to my right hand,
> I find no friend by my side;
> no way of escape is in sight,
> no one comes to rescue me.

He cries unrestrainedly to God, his refuge and portion in the land of the living, craving for relief from those who harass him, begging to be set free from prison, one of inner hell as much as outer incarceration. Then he can praise God's name, while the righteous crown him with honour as they witness his due reward.

There is a shade of difference between despair and desperation. While in both there is a loss, or else an utter want, of hope, the despairing person is filled with despair whereas the one who is desperate is moved by his despair. And so the individual may resort to reckless behaviour as a last response to the apparently hopeless situation around him. He moves to the periphery of the normal agencies of succour, whether medical, legal or spiritual. He will clutch at the least available straw in a last attempt to escape drowning. And so it is that quite a few psalms are dominated by feelings of desperation, since the writer is an active person and not merely a passive animal. Unrestrained anger at the inscrutable ways of the God who so often hides himself from the pain of human experience helps to assuage the intolerable emptiness of total despair.

Quite a number of the psalms contain passages of anger of such vehemence that they embarrass, and not occasionally shock, the reader who has known the Christian revelation of love as the supreme manifestation of God's dealings with his creatures here on earth. Nevertheless, before such a reader assumes the mantle of a superior spiritual guide, it will do him good to understand the historical perspective of the Psalmist and also, even more pertinently, the inner workings of his own psyche. How easy it is to judge and condemn when one can sit in peace and assurance! And Jesus sharply reminds us, we too have to bear the humiliation of being ushered away from the better seats of the banquet that we had chosen and brought to less impressive places, where we may eat with those whom we would previously have regarded with distaste, if not contempt. The end of Jesus' own life was spent in the close company of two such individuals, all bound for a common death, as are we also at the end of this life's journey. A question mark hangs over us all; we do not know from where we came or for what region we are bound. An inner spark within us tells us that there is some tremendous meaning behind the rational enigma, and the light of this spark has to be followed if we are not to go insane at the apparent futility, to say nothing of the manifest injustice, of life as we find it on a purely superficial level. It is not unreasonable, and certainly not unforgivable, that we from time to time explode emotionally under the strain. God forgives even when the human cannot do so spontaneously; indeed were it not for this love that is the nature of the Deity, none of us would be alive. The allegory of the Flood in Genesis 6–8 would have been repeated so often that eventually no person would have been found to assume the saving character of Noah.

It is in this frame of mind that the passages of anger, and especially those of fierce imprecation (cursing), are to be read with quiet sympathy and not supercilious judgement. It is right that they should be avoided in public worship, for they might possibly inflame the passions of an already emotionally unstable attender, and lead him to desperate action. Likewise we should come before God in chaste simplicity and quiet regard in order to be filled with the good things he has prepared for us. But before we can receive these gifts in perfect awareness and full dedication, we have to discharge our sinfulness to God, who alone can receive our foulness as a sacrifice and transmute it to health through his unspeakably great love. Thus a general confession is a vital part of communal no less than private worship, and the psalms of anger and imprecation help us to look into our own darkness and acknowledge it in the company of the ancient Psalmist. Times may change, but human nature remains distressingly selfish until the direct impress of God's presence had been registered on it.

It is a passion for justice, at least as an individual sees and seeks it, that inspires the dark, inflammatory passages of the psalms. The human soul will, like the inexorably persistent widow described in Luke 18:1–5, demand justice. Even if the judge is hard and dishonest she will wear him down with her nagging; but, as the parable tells us, God is perpetually giving justice to his chosen, to whom he listens with patience as they cry without ceasing. Their relief is assured, but then comes the challenging question: when the Son of Man comes will he find faith on earth? He is in fact the justice we all seek, but in him a purely legalistic satisfaction is transcended in a love that is able to forgive spontaneously. This is the end of the process, but we cannot grasp at it until we have learnt to accept ourselves and the world and work for its healing. Justice is not supplanted until it has done it cleansing work, which is to expose evil and corruption and bring all culprits to the seat of judgement. It is only then that the higher law of love can assert itself, so that healing may end the process of humiliation and suffering of victim and offender alike.

A notorious call for vengeance ends the otherwise beautiful Psalm 137, which begins:

> By the rivers of Babylon we sat down and wept
> as we remembered Zion.
> On the willow tree there
> we hung up our lyres,
> for those who had carried us captive
> asked us to sing them a song,
> our captors called on us to be joyful:
> 'Sing us one of the songs of Zion.'

But how could they sing the Lord's song in a foreign land? The writer goes on to pledge a complete sacrifice of his body if he fails to remember and honour Jerusalem. And then follows a call for vengeance on the Edomites, who joined forces with the Babylonians in the final sack of the city and called for its total destruction. The climax reaches its zenith

in an imprecation against the Babylonians themselves for
their destructiveness:

> Babylon, Babylon the destroyer,
> happy is he who repays you
> for what you did to us!

Then comes the terrible sentiment, 'Happy is he who seizes
your babes and dashes them against a rock.' Before we condemn this utterly, it must be recalled that the law of *talio*, as
laid down in Exodus 21:23–25, required a stringently exact
punishment for the offence committed against the person.
Primitive as it sounds to us, it was in fact an advance on the
savage vengeance visited on offenders previous to the Law as
expounded by Moses. As the Jews grew in spiritual understanding after their return from Babylonian exile, so their
interpretation of the Law became more humane, until the
advent of Jesus who brought the concept of forgiveness to its
highest point. It is nevertheless important to understand that
Christ's work of love had been well prepared by the spiritual
leaders who preceded him. He is to be seen as the final
fulfilment of the Law and not its supplanter, let alone its
destroyer (Matt. 5:17–19).

Psalm 58, directed at unjust rulers who abuse their power
and judge their people unfairly, contains a long passage of
imprecation: God is urged to destroy them utterly so that it
may be as if they had never been born. The final exultation
is sincere if vicious:

> The righteous will rejoice at the sight of the vengeance
>   done;
> they will bathe their feet in the blood of the wicked.
> It will be said,
> 'There is after all reward for the righteous;
> there is after all a God who dispenses justice on earth.'

Nothing is in fact more terrible than the apparent victory
of the forces of evil over common decency in any generation.
The virtually unopposed advance of Nazism in the thirties,

the world at large blinding itself to the atrocities committed in Germany, is a case in point. Even more subtle was the era of Stalinism in Russia that was so easily cloaked under the impressive façade of social justice for the masses, while all sparks of individual protest were ruthlessly extinguished. When one remembers such events in our own century and the millions of innocent people who were savagely murdered, the strength of abhorrence registered in this psalm becomes less repulsive. But its impotence remains until justice is vindicated.

Psalm 55, a prayer to God in persecution, starts by arresting God's attention in urgent stress:

> Listen, God, to my prayer:
> do not hide yourself from my pleading.
> Hear me and give me an answer,
> for my cares leave me no peace.

The writer is panic-stricken by the clamour of his enemies, his heart is torn with anguish while his body trembles with fear:

> I say: 'Oh that I had the wings of a dove
> to fly away and find rest!
> I would escape far away
> to a refuge in the wilderness.

The Psalmist's particular woe is that an intimate friend has betrayed him, so that the very meaning of his life has been torn asunder. One thinks of the betrayal of David by his trusted counsellor Ahithophel, who deserted to Absalom the royal mutineer. When his subversive advice was disregarded he committed suicide. In a somewhat different circumstance Christ's apostle Judas Iscariot was to betray his master to the hands of sinners, but here it was Jesus' innocence that was to cause Judas so intense a remorse that he summarily killed himself. The Psalmist contents himself with repeated imprecations against his persecutors while he prays earnestly for God to help in the morning, noonday and evening, which are the established hours of prayer. It is fascinating how entreaty to God alternates with imprecation against the adversary:

> May death strike them,
> may they go down alive to Sheol;
> for their homes are haunts of evil!

Even at the end the two recurring themes show themselves in strength:

> Commit your fortunes to the Lord,
> and he will sustain you;
> he will never let the righteous be shaken.
> But you will cast them down, God,
> into the pit of destruction;
> bloodthirsty and treacherous,
> they will not live out half their days.
> For my part, Lord, I shall put my trust in you.

It would seem that the desperation that followed the onslaught of immense powers of darkness was assuaged by a full acknowledgement of the situation in the presence of God. It is only in the divine presence that we can be fully ourselves; what would seem revolting to our fellows is acceptable to our Father, no doubt with the best of humour. We remember the unjudging reception of the publican in the famous parable (Luke 18:9–14) and also the welcome home given to the Prodigal Son (Luke 15:11–32).

The Psalmist's anxiety of God's delay in coming to his help in a time of trial is another form of darkness. Psalm 44 is a classical development of this theme that has national rather than merely personal implications. The first eight verses commemorate God's saving work in the past that culminated in the settlement in Canaan, but then follows a long complaint about the present distress. The nation is subjugated under foreign domination, for God no longer leads the Israelite army. It is as if God sold his people for next to nothing and yet made no profit from the transaction. All that remains is mockery and abuse. But the nub of the matter follows in verse 17: 'Though all this has befallen us, we do not forget you and have not been false to your covenant.' There has been no apostasy, and yet the punishment of God's indifference is as if he had crushed the nation personally.

> Had we forgotten the name of our God
> and spread out our hands in prayer to alien gods,
> would not God have found out,
> for he knows the secrets of the heart.
> For your sake we are being done to death all day long,
> treated like sheep for slaughter.

One wonders when the people had been as innocent as this; the pre-exilic community had continued to sin despite the warnings of various prophets. The exiles who were allowed to return by Cyrus the Persian king formed a chastened group, and perhaps their affliction under the hellenizing king Antiochus Epiphanes during the Maccabaean period formed the historical background for at least this portion of the psalm.

A similar type of situation is contained in Psalm 89. The first thirty-eight verses celebrate God's love and faithfulness to his chosen people, which culminated in the promise made to the greatest Israelite king through the prophet Nathan:

> I have found David my servant
> and anointed him with my sacred oil.
> My hand will be ready to help him,
> my arm to give him strength.

There is the warning, after Nathan's prophecy, of punishment for disobedience, but an overall assurance of the continuing divine love and faithfulness. Then follows in verse 39 a recital of a complete reversal of fortune, and the psalm ends:

> Remember, Lord, the taunts hurled at your servant,
> how I have borne in my heart the calumnies of the
>   nations;

46

for your enemies have taunted us, Lord,
taunted your anointed king at every step.

The writer asks God how long he will hide himself, how long
will his wrath blaze like a fire. He reminds God of the fleeting
nature of human life, and asks whether he has created all
humanity to no purpose.

The dark dread of misfortune cuts us also down to size. In
the gloom we seem to be completely isolated, for few friends
can stand this strain for long. Even Jesus' three companions
could not stay fully awake for one hour as their Master strove
with the accumulated sin of the world. In Gethsemane he
knew the feeling of total dereliction as he had to struggle on
alone. His assumption of this desolation has made it easier
for us to bear, because he is with us in our travail, and
alongside us as he brings our misery to the Father. By this I
mean that we, in our distress, can call upon God in a very
personal way. Like the Suffering Servant of Isaiah 53:

He was despised, shunned by all,
pain-racked and afflicted by disease;
we despised him, we held him of no account,
an object from which people turn away their eyes.
Yet it was our afflictions he was bearing,
our pain he endured;
while we thought of him as smitten by God,
struck down by disease and misery.

We may trust that Christ assumes our anger, irritation,
anxiety and frustration and brings them to the Father. Even
the imprecations which we may from time to time mutter
under our breath are taken up with good humour by the Son,
who then presents them, on our behalf, as a sacrifice fit for
God in his glory and love. Only so are they healed and given
back to us for further use.

We may end this chapter on a somewhat lighter note. In
Psalm 139, noted in detail on page 11, the writer is so jealous
for God's reputation that he allies himself in his enthusiasm

47

to the Almighty to the extent of supporting, if not protecting, him.

> How I hate those that hate you, Lord!
> I loath those who defy you;
> I hate them with undying hatred;
> I reckon them my own enemies.

This pledge of absolute loyalty is as touching as it is commendable. Our problem lies in being able to discern the Holy Spirit's work in our individual lives. The history of religion contains far too many examples of irrational fervour that culminated in persecutions and murders. A theocracy may in theory have God in charge. In practice, his creatures take control in his name. The harm done to God's name is frequently irremediable, at least in the short term. It seems that the Almighty is well able to get about his own business; what he wants of us is a reflection of his own love and faithfulness.

6

Assurance When Afraid

The Lord is my light and my salvation;
whom should I fear?
The Lord is the stronghold of my life;
of whom then should I go in dread?

So begin the beautiful words of Psalm 27. The Psalmist goes on to observe that when he is attacked by evildoers, identified as his adversaries and enemies, it is they who are discomfited; even the threat of an army encamped against him would not cause him any fear, not even the assault of armed men. Following this affirmation of faith, the writer craves to know his Lord with increasing intimacy. He knows that in God alone lie succour and shelter, in his Master there is triumph over his assailants so that he can hold his head high and sing a psalm of praise.

Then comes an abrupt change of mood; from triumphant assurance there is a desperate plea for help against present attack: his faith now has to be put to the test of action as he battles for his very life. Knowing that alone he will be exterminated, he calls desperately to God, begging him not to turn away from him in his wrath or to reject and forsake him in his extremity. The apparent result is survival, perhaps even victory, for in the end he affirms his trust in God:

Well I know that I shall see the goodness of the Lord
in the land of the living.
Wait for the Lord; be strong and brave;
and put your hope in the Lord.

The outcome has by no means been easy, let alone a foregone conclusion, but in the heat of the fight wisdom has come to the Psalmist as he asked God to teach him his way, a request so often encountered in the psalms, especially Psalm 119 which, as we have seen, is one extended praise of the divine law and a plea for help in realizing it in one's personal life.

The first six verses of Psalm 27, those of confident assurance, have often been on the lips of people in the midst of trouble. Long ago I read of a woman who was one of the first to undergo surgery on her ovaries. There were no anaesthetics in those days, and so she kept up her courage, incredible in terms of our own times, by repeating verses from the Psalms; these verses from Psalm 27 have been a special strength in extreme travail, for they speak of the universal human experience. They also are an epitome of religious faith that has later to be tested in a time of trouble. The abrupt change in the Psalmist's tone as he is challenged is typical of the human condition; we at once revert to our childhood state, which is never very far from the surface of our consciousness no matter how sophisticated our worldly attitude, and call desperately for our beloved parents' presence and assistance; in the process humbling ourselves sufficiently to ask for guidance and vowing to start a new style of living.

When the emergency is over most of us tend to revert to the past heedless existence, a situation so dramatically described in the parable of the Unforgiving Debtor (Matt. 18:23–35). As in this fearsome story, we lay up for ourselves suffering out of all proportion to what we knew previously. But a few of us, perhaps by virtue of rueful experience in the past, have learnt the lesson of gratitude, and our lives are turned more positively to the light. This is the full meaning of conversion. The courageous Christian woman in the agony of primitive surgery had already attained this level of spiritual awareness, and so she could cooperate with God and the gallant surgeon. The end result was not only her own cure, a minor landmark in medical history, but an opening of the way to further surgical expertise which has culminated so magnificently in the wonderful technical triumphs of the present day.

A rather similar affirmation of God's presence is contained in Psalm 11:

> In the Lord I take refuge. How can you say to me,
> 'Flee like a bird to the mountains;
> for see, the wicked string their bows,
> and fit the arrow to the bowstring,
> to shoot from the darkness at honest folk'?

Here there is little to fear because the Psalmist's confidence is high. Being of considerable integrity he can trust the Almighty without reserve, and play his part alongside God in routing the designs of the wicked.

> The Lord is in his holy temple;
> the Lord's throne is in heaven.
> His gaze is upon mankind, his searching eye tests them.

The writer sees God weighing the just and the unjust, hating all those who inflict violence but loving just dealing and turning his face towards the upright. The assurance is distinctly warmer than in Psalm 27. The Psalmist may have recently been blessed with a victory over adverse circumstances, and so been able to accept more readily God's concern with the world.

When we know God we encounter love, for that is his nature. In love there is no room for fear; indeed perfect love banishes fear (1 John 4:18). We may learn about God by diligently studying the Bible, but in the end a true knowledge of the Lord does not follow a detailed reading of any written teaching. He is known best while we are constantly aware of the world around us in the present moment, for it is thus that we are in clear-cut relationship with the Deity. He gives us his essence while we open ourselves in trust to his divine providence and the service of all those around us.

There are two modalities of fear: an instinctive fear of the Creator and his inscrutable power and a fear of the circumstances of life itself. This usually shows itself more starkly in unpleasant situations, such as those we have read about in the two psalms. The fear that confronts us, as a nameless awe in the face of the terrible mystery of God, is slowly softened and warmed by the love which we know as we come closer to him in prayer and in humble service. Furthermore when we know the unconditional embrace of God's loving presence we are able to confront the world's dangers with a calm restraint, quite unlike the usual consternation of which we are only too well acquainted. All this of course is a slowly developing process, since we inhabit a very earthy physical body which flinches from any situation that might lead to its injury and possible destruction. And yet if we proceed with the assurance that is the fruit of answered prayer, the very heart of earnest faith, our body may learn intuitively of a life that reaches beyond the earth to glorious plains beyond. We may recall here Ezekiel's vision of a plain of dead bones that he resurrected to full life as an immense human army under the command of God (Ezek. 37:1–14).

It is a good practice to recite portions of the psalms when all is chaos around us. They have a remarkably cleansing effect on the inner side of the cup of life, so that finally the outer rim is also cleansed (Matt. 23:25–26). In other words, when we are inwardly renewed the process extends to the outer situation also.

A further side to the human response to fear in the light of God's eternal beneficence is contained in Psalm 56. Here the Psalmist bewails his present condition: trampled underfoot, harassed by his assailants and oppressed by his numerous enemies:

> In my day of fear,
> I put my trust in you, the Most High,
> in God, whose promise is my boast,
> in God I trust and shall not be afraid;
> what can mortals do to me?

He then returns to his first theme, describing the malice of his foes, and this line of thought is succeeded by an inner assurance that God knows his grief. Therefore the Almighty should come speedily to his succour.

> This I know, that God is on my side.
> In God, whose promise is my boast . . .
> in God I trust and shall not be afraid;
> what can mortals do to me?

The psalm ends with the continued oscillation between articulated trust and a fear at the hostility of those close to the writer. The words of confidence seem to be a recitation aimed, albeit unconsciously, at raising the Psalmist's spirits during the time of anxiety when peril lurks at every corner. In a time of action doubt could be fatal; we have to do the right thing now even when we are far from sure what that right thing is. It is in this frame of mind that our constant awareness of God and our conversation with him can be of great help. One cannot but smile at the writer's belief that God is on his side. In times gone by it was easier to assign the divine assistance to one party more than another, depending, of course, on one's own loyalty and concern. We have had to learn by the bitter fruits of wars and lesser conflicts that God is on everybody's side – which is a more positive way of affirming the divine neutrality in human conflict. It is we who have to use the help given by God; the virtuous, by their life of simplicity and discipline, will be closer to that help than those who use it profligately. This seems to be the way in which conflicts are brought to a satisfactory conclusion.

If we can be quiet and commend ourselves to our Maker, albeit in quaking trust that seeks to override a more basic fear, he will be close to us and we may rest assured as we relax in his presence. So much is assured us in Psalm 91, one of the most famous psalms and a regular reading at compline. It is indeed good to retire to sleep with some of its sentences on our lips and in our mind.

> He who lives in the shelter of the Most High,
> who lodges under the shadow of the Almighty,

says of the Lord, 'He is my refuge and fortress,
my God in whom I put my trust.'

There is no savage attack by ferocious animals or the inroads
of lethal diseases that need frighten the worshipper, for God
will cover him with his wings, granting refuge under his
pinions, while his truth will be a shield to ward off all evil
assaults. No terror, whether plague or vicious assault, can
come near him, despite the extermination of many people
beside him. Indeed he will have the privilege of witnessing
the retribution that is visited on the evildoer. One remembers
the temptations of Jesus in the wilderness after his baptism
and the full awakening of the Holy Spirit within him. In Luke
4:10–11 the devil quotes from this psalm to the effect that, if
Jesus is really the Son of God, he should be able to throw
himself down from the parapet of the Temple:

For he will charge his angels
to guard you wherever you go.
to lift you on their hands
for fear you strike your foot against a stone.

Jesus in turn makes the crucial quotation from Deuteronomy
6:16, to the effect that one must not put the Lord our God to
the test, as did the Israelites at Massah (Exod. 17:1–7). The
wonderful account of Jesus' temptation in the wilderness
(Matt. 4:1–11 with the parallel record in Luke 4:1–13) gives
an example of Scripture mischievously quoted and its correction by the more enlightened use of appropriate texts.

The psalm ends with a promise of deliverance from trouble
because he loves his Lord and knows his name. This knowledge is one of intimate fellowship, not merely intellectual
assent such as may conclude a theological debate. We remember that God gives us no name; 'I am that I am' is what
Moses is told, and he is to tell the Israelites that I am has
sent him to them. But he is also the God of their forefathers,
Abraham, Isaac and Jacob (Exod. 3:14–15). In other words
the Most High cannot be named, for if he were he could be
controlled by his creatures. Our name defines and limits us,

whereas God has no limitation and can be known only by his outflowing, uncreated energies, which are light and love.

It is noteworthy also that God promises his presence in time of trouble. The divine assistance does not exempt even the most devout saint from suffering, but it promises its support. The travail of Jesus at Gethsemane and on the cross at Calvary substantiates this truth, except that in his extremity Jesus felt completely bereft of his Father's presence as he cried aloud the first verse of Psalm 22. But he was nevertheless sustained; as we read in Hebrews 5:7–10, in the course of his life on earth he offered up prayers and petitions, with great wailing, to God who alone was able to deliver him from death. His devotion ensured that his prayer was heard; though he was Son, he had to learn obedience through his travail, and, once perfected for the work he had to do, he became the source of eternal salvation for all who obey him. He was now qualified to bear the mysterious eternal priesthood of the order of Melchizedek.

In an infinitely smaller way this is our destiny also as we pass through the shadowland of fear.

> When he calls to me, I shall answer;
> I shall be with him in time of trouble;
> I shall rescue him and bring him to honour,
> I shall satisfy him with long life
> and show him my salvation.

These thoughts finally bring us to another favourite psalm, small in size but massive in content. The opening lines of Psalm 23 need no introduction:

> The Lord is my shepherd; I lack for nothing.
> He makes me lie down in green pastures,
> he leads me to water where I may rest;
> he revives my spirit;
> for his name's sake he guides me in the right paths.

The image of the good shepherd, first completely outlined in Ezekiel 34:11–16 and authoritatively fulfilled in the person of

Christ (John 10:1–18), is beautifully revealed here; the Psalmist goes on to affirm God's unceasing presence even if he were to walk through an impenetrably dark valley. This presence is no mere cipher, but, to quote Isaiah 40:29:

> He gives vigour to the weary,
> new strength to the exhausted.

The basis of this help lies in the second image contained in the psalm, that of the host at the heavenly banquet:

> You spread a table for me in the presence of my
>   enemies;
> you have richly anointed my head with oil,
> and my cup brims over.

In God's care we are filled with heavenly strength; our enemies could be likewise filled, but they have chosen to rely on their own resources. It is important to affirm that the Creator loves all his creatures equally, because this is the very nature of love; or as Peter was told in the matter of his baptism of the gentile centurion Cornelius, God has no favourites (Acts 10:34). It would indeed be a sorry day if our Lord bestowed his generosity on only a small élite who were saved, while all the others went away empty. But until one is humble, freed from all self-assertiveness, one cannot partake of the food on the heavenly table. This consists of love in its various earthly forms that are ultimately to be resurrected to the life eternal in the form of the great lover, whom Christians see in the person of Jesus Christ.

The situation is completely revealed in the occasion and the words of the Magnificat (Luke 1:53):

> He has filled the hungry with good things,
> and sent the rich away empty.

And so the Psalmist can be sure of goodness and unfailing love all the days of his life, while dwelling unassailably in God's house. This house can be seen in a triple mode of private dwelling, the Church, and the whole created universe. How then should we behave when we are afraid, when fear gnaws at the very roots of our existence? We should not be ashamed to admit our fears, trying as much as possible to get to their basis on a rational level. And then we should, like the Psalmist, offer them up to God in silent prayer. There is encouragement in Psalm 37:25:

> I have been young and now have grown old,
> but never have I seen the righteous forsaken
> or their children begging bread.

In the short term this dictum is often disproved, but if we are patient and never cease to put our trust in God, we shall ultimately know victory. The writers of the psalms experienced similar emotions to ours, hence the long-lasting value of these pieces of religious poetry to us, even 2,500 to 3,000 years later. If we can proceed to settle down in the depth of the soul, seen anatomically as the centre of the abdomen and radiating to the heart, we shall learn of an inner strength that accompanies us through all the trials of life. And then the complete assurance of God's presence and assistance in Psalms 23 and 91 will become something more than picturesque poetry. And thus we may proceed on our life's journey with emotions alternating from those of Psalm 27 and Psalm 56 to the greater and more positive assertions and affirmations of Psalm 11.

Life is a fluctuating affair; as in Psalm 27, we must expect periods of anxiety to follow joyful moods of elation at the sheer splendour of existence. But if we hold on, the cloud of fear will eventually lift and reveal a heavenly landscape in which a general harmony is able to comprehend all dissonant elements. These too play their part in the vast tapestry of life.

7

In Times of Trouble

> God is our refuge and our stronghold,
> a timely help in trouble.

So begin the familiar words of Psalm 46. The Psalmist is confident of God's help in all calamities, whether climatic or national. The first image suggests a gigantic earthquake with an accompanying storm at sea; the second a national emergency when the Holy City is attacked by vast enemy forces and all is set for disaster. It is probable that the writer had in mind the siege of Jerusalem by the Assyrian army under Sennacherib in 701 BC:

> There is a river whose streams bring joy to the city of
>   God,
> the holy dwelling of the Most High;
> God is in her midst; she will not be overthrown,
> and at break of day he will help her.

In the psalms generally, dawn is the time of the divine favour whereas evening heralds the time of trial and suffering. And so the people of Israel can rest in the Lord's protection even when chaos reigns around them.

> Come, see what the Lord has done,
> the astounding deeds he has wrought on earth.

The writer exults in the power of the Almighty to end wars and destroy the weapons of battle. And so comes the celebrated tenth verse:

Let be then; learn that I am God.

The translation found in the Authorized Version is more poetic, 'Be still, and know that I am God', but it seems to emphasize the divine indwelling in a way that is incompatible with the understanding of God that is typical of the Old Testament. The divine immanence is an article of faith of mystical religion; indeed it is faith that has been fertilized by knowledge. But the God of the Old Testament is severely transcendent, even when, as in the prophecy of Hosea, the Lord stands close to his people and weeps over their apostasies and longs to enfold them in the embrace of forgiveness. The more modern translation of this famous verse is apposite if less picturesque.

What the Psalmist is telling us is that we should relax in times of national no less than cosmic disaster, and put our trust in the Lord. This is not a shallow abdication of duty nor an abject admission of total impotence in the face of a present emergency. It is to be seen rather as a realistic appraisal of the situation and a giving of ourself in dark faith to God, to do as he shows us instead of becoming stricken with panic and thus adding our quota to the prevailing confusion. This lesson is of universal application, being as appropriate in personal strife as in national upheaval.

Psalm 37, in which the fates of the virtuous and the wicked are compared in the rather cut and dried manner of the early Wisdom literature enunciates a similar doctrine in the seventh verse:

> Wait quietly for the Lord, be patient till he comes:
> do not envy those who gain their ends,
> or be vexed at their success.

This verse has again been translated more poetically in the Authorized Version:

> Rest in the Lord, and wait patiently for him:
> fret not thyself because of him who prospereth in his
> way,

because of the man who bringeth wicked devices to
pass.

Waiting quietly perhaps does not have that sense of complete
submission that rest might imply, but it reminds us that we
too have to play our part. An inert type of rest can easily
degenerate into frank sloth – leaving it all to God. But if we
wait in alert patience, we will know what to do both immediately and in that future moment when direct action is
required.

Returning to Psalm 46, we learn about God by considering
his works in creation. As St Paul says in Romans 1:19–20, all
that can be known of God lies open to our unclouded intellect
in surveying the created order around us. On the other hand
we know God by an act of union with him. This comes by
divine grace, a totally unmerited gift from God to his rational
creature, and we are, as it were, taken up into the presence
of our Lord, there to be enwrapped in a light too powerful to
be borne by earthly eyes and a love so intense that no part
of our being is exempted from its embrace. The result of this
completely unexpected infusion of the divine grace is that we
become changed creatures, remade, albeit ever so slightly, in
the image of God which was our original stature in the divine
mind, and is, through Christ, to become our final end. This
intimate knowledge of God is prefigured in the perfect union
of the holy spouses of antiquity, which gave birth to children
of promise: Isaac, Samson, Samuel and John the Baptist. It
is improbable that the Psalmist had any such thought when
he wrote Psalm 46.

Nevertheless an appreciation of the divine indwelling in the
soul of all of us can add a fresh dimension of truth to the
Psalmist's inspiration. The city mentioned in the fourth verse
is even more pertinently our own soul than holy Jerusalem
itself, and the divine presence is within it. The river whose
streams bring it joy is the Holy Spirit with its overflowing
power. We recall the lovely meeting of Jesus and the Samaritan woman at Jacob's well described in the fourth chapter of
St John's Gospel. Jesus compares the water from the well
that quenches human thirst for only a little while with the

water he can give. This is as a spring of water within us that wells up and brings eternal life. The simple woman can envisage this water in material terms only, but Jesus hints that a renewed style of living is first required before the great inner transformation can occur. The time will come when true worship is quite independent of locality but is an inner offering to God from the soul: God is spirit, and he must be worshipped in spirit and in truth. When one is truly still, one is made aware of the divine presence within; when one lets be and does not interfere with matters or proceed to do anything, the inner silence, perhaps appreciated for the first time in one's life, leads one to the still, small voice within that is the source of eternal wisdom. And then one can start to do what ought to be done rather than what one would like to have done.

In his teaching on prayer Jesus tells us to go into a private room with shut doors. There we know God in the secret place, and he can be fully accessible to us, so that a conversation of great meaning can take place (Matt. 6:6). He goes on to remind us that we do not need elaborate words but rather quiet listening, for our Father already knows what we need. The Lord's Prayer which follows, with its familiar clauses, is designed to show us what we need essentially for immediate health and eternal sustenance. First there is a lifting up of our eyes to God in his majesty and then a heartfelt desire that God's kingdom may come on earth also. We then pray for our immediate material needs – a day's supply is enough at a time lest we become so preoccupied with mundane things that we overlook our spiritual work. After this we remember our deeper condition, needing both forgiveness and the capacity to pardon those who have hurt us. Finally comes the conflict with evil; the devil (however we may picture this malign principle) will tempt us to put our Creator to the test, as he did Jesus in the three temptations in the wilderness that inaugurated his great ministry after his baptism. The tendency to use God for our own ends, no matter how laudable these may appear, is a constant hazard of the spiritual life. Once we use God in this proprietorial way, we lie fully open to the assaults of evil influences. We need the ever-present divine assistance to direct our eyes away from ourself to the mystery of God himself in constant prayer, worship and service. It is thus that we are delivered from the evil one. The optional doxology at the end has the virtue of bringing us finally in praise of the divine glory.

All this inner dialogue goes on in the depth of the soul, aptly compared with a private room whose doors are shut. If the doors are left open, the conversation will be interrupted by the various thoughts that usually stream through the mind, inducing vague anxiety that shows itself in a worrying that simply interferes with the smooth conduct of praying, as it does also the outer tenor of our life. Since God knows our needs before we ask for help, is it sensible to commend them to him? The answer is emphatically in the affirmative, for when we speak directly, whether aloud or in mental discourse, we focus our problems in the divine presence, and, once we are able to be quiet and listen, we will learn many truths, thereby finding surprising answers to our manifold problems. God meets us on our own level, and, provided we are willing, will lead us to his holy habitation, the heavenly form on which the Holy City is modelled. Thus Moses was told to work to the design he had been shown on Mount Sinai (Exod. 25:40). When, like Moses, we are lifted up to God, our attention is riveted on his presence, and the door of the soul is effectively shut to all distraction. It may need an impending calamity of the type mentioned in Psalm 46 to bring us to such a complete submission to God's presence, so that we may at last see the truth of our situation and the means of our healing.

When one thinks of Psalm 46 on an historical level, one cannot help recalling that the confidence the writer had in God's overall protection of Holy Zion in the face of the remarkable retreat of the Assyrian forces at the very gates of Jerusalem was not to be confirmed later on. About a century later the city and its Temple were to be destroyed by the Babylonians. The Israelites were so confident about the inviolability of these places that they presumed on the automatic protection of God despite their continual apostasies. Jeremiah had warned them about the error of assuming the

Temple could not be destroyed (Jer. 7:1–7). Only an amended way of life would ensure the survival of the country, but this message they would not heed. One can learn from this that the time of total reliance upon God is short, indeed bounded entirely by the period of emergency. But once this has lifted, active cooperation with the divine presence is necessary. It was the survivors of the Babylonian exile who showed this understanding in their lives as they proceeded painfully to rebuild the Temple and repair the city walls. If we do not work constructively with the law of life, we shall soon be destroyed. There is a time for patient retrenchment, but this is succeeded by active outflowing in the Spirit of God. It is one thing to rely on the divine assistance, but quite another to take that help for granted. The first is an active cooperation, the second a negligent acceptance with neither gratitude nor commitment to future work for the Kingdom.

The situation mirrored in Psalm 13 is a more personal affliction in the face of persistent attacks by the writer's enemies. He asks how long God will leave him forgotten, hiding, as it were, his face from him, while his soul is in anguish and grief overwhelms his heart. He beseeches God to respond to his suffering lest his adversaries gloat over him. But then comes the answer that is repeated by the Psalmist:

> As for me, I trust in your unfailing love;
> my heart will rejoice when I am brought to safety.
> I shall sing to the Lord, for he has granted all my desire.

This seems to be something more than mere hope welling up in his heart, simply wishful thinking. There is a direct message to the mind from the depth of the soul, in whose most sacred point, which we may call the spirit, the divine presence lies immanent. As we have already noted, such a view about God is basically alien to the Old Testament – and to many ardent theists also, who see the human being as too corrupt by virtue of 'original sin' to have any innate communication with God – and yet it cannot be suppressed in the writer's personal experience, no matter how he may choose to disguise or disown it. The psalm has a glorious trust about it; in his mind the writer can already envisage relief. This is an example of hope made real by faith, whose end is positive action initiated by God and effected by the human. Another way of putting this observation is that of Hebrews 11:1: faith gives substance to our hopes and convinces us of realities we do not see. At the right time that 'substance', that tangible proof in the world of matter, will show itself in remarkable events around us.

At the time of writing, one cannot but look in amazement at the changed political situation in Eastern Europe, where, without force of arms, freedom has dawned for vast populations whose lives would have seemed to be indefinitely encompassed by ideological dogmatism and international isolation. Trust and prayer over the decades have worked to change human awareness; discernment is now what is most required.

Psalm 103, one of the loveliest of the 150, is a hymn of praise to God's love even in the midst of human dereliction. It is a glorious psalm to repeat when all seems to be going wrong, and life itself is a mockery, 'a tale told by an idiot, full of sound and fury, signifying nothing', as Shakespeare puts it in *Macbeth*. When we have borne the full impact of our trial, silence may at last take the stage, as it did when the debate between Job and his friends ended on a note of human futility and intellectual impotence. Then at last we are drawn to the basic issues of our existence: the privilege of life, the glory of humanity and the amazing gift of being able to know God in intimate communion and to trace his ways in investigating the many prodigies of nature. To lose ourself in the marvel of creation is the way to freeing ourself of the present anguish with its threat of future chaos. Indeed, how easy it is to succumb to our own affliction when we could call so easily on the God of love for immediate relief and later healing!

> Bless the Lord, my soul;
> with all my being I bless his holy name.
> Bless the Lord, my soul,
> and forget none of his benefits.

He pardons all my wrongdoing
and heals all my ills.

The Psalmist revels in describing the divine mercy and compassion. His patience is as unceasing as his faithfulness, his
leniency is a measure of his great love for his erring rational
creature, the human being.

As a father has compassion on his children,
so the Lord has compassion on those who fear him;
for he knows how we were made;
he remembers that we are but dust.

The fear that is such an integral part of the Wisdom literature of the Bible is a deep respect for God and all he has
made. It is a compound of awe in the face of the tremendous
mystery underlying creation and a deep concern for the wellbeing and maintenance of all that has been created. When
Moses encountered God in the burning bush, he was told not
to come near and to take off his sandals, for he was standing
on holy ground. Moses hid his face, being afraid to look on
God (Exod. 3:2–6). Though the Almighty dwarfed Moses and
could have destroyed him in a trice, instead he told him to
come close to him on the holy ground. He was to remove his
footwear, a symbol of earthly possessions, and enter fully into
physical as well as spiritual communion with his Creator.
This account gives us some idea of awe before God and
the marvellous downpouring of his grace upon his obedient
creature.

With great poignancy the Psalmist contrasts human transience with the everlasting love of God. The words about the
human condition are especially striking, and account in part
for the frequent use of this psalm at funeral and thanksgiving
services:

The days of a mortal are as grass;
he blossoms like a wild flower in the meadow:
a wind passes over him, and he is gone,
and his place knows him no more.

Indeed when we remember how frantically our friends strove for their living, their families and their reputations, how proud they were of their possessions, how quick to become angry at even small reverses of fortune, we can only smile indulgently at the evanescence of human endeavour in face of the great mystery.

The unlimited, unconditional love expressed in Psalm 103 makes it an apt prefiguration both of St John's teaching in 1 John 3 and 4:7–21, and that of Christ the incarnate Word himself. He too underwent the painful death of a human, and within a few days he would have been equally forgotten had he not risen from the dead and revealed a completely new pattern of existence to his amazed disciples, and through them to the whole world.

When we are deeply in trouble and no rational solution seems acceptable, we may indeed call upon the Lord, using whatever name seems fit to us. The subsequent strengthening will fill us, of whatever traditional background, with the resolve to go steadfastly onward looking towards the light ahead of us. As Jesus warned his followers, no one setting his hand to the plough and then looking back is fit for God's kingdom (Luke 9:62).

Psalm 103 also reminds us of the indivisible fellowship of all God's creatures:

Bless the Lord, you his angels,
mighty in power, who do his bidding
and obey his command.
Bless the Lord, all you his hosts,
his ministers who do his will.
Bless the Lord, all created things,
everywhere in his dominion.
Bless the Lord, my soul.

We work with the immense ministry of angels and the glorious Communion of Saints for the coming of God's kingdom on earth. The saints too knew their times of trouble when they lived among us.

8

Suffering and its Reward

Our life cannot avoid the experience of suffering, for by it
alone do we move from a rather comfortable, if not complacent, view of the world around us to a deeper knowledge
of ourself. Job himself, a perfectly righteous man, had to come
to terms with the darkness within himself, concealed by a
defence of laudable philanthropy, before he could be guided
into a more adult understanding of the God he so reverently
worshipped. And so he confessed to his three friends who had
come to comfort him, 'Every terror that haunted me has
caught up with me; what I dreaded has overtaken me' (Job
3:25). He learnt much about the true nature of suffering and
its latent blessing even during his fruitless debate with his
companions; the end was a direct awareness of the immeasurable glory of the Creator, compared with which his own
travail was as nothing. This is the consolation we all may
know provided we persist onwards even when faith itself
seems a tragic delusion. We know God primarily as a presence
within us, or at least in direct contact with the core of our
being. But life is here to make that intimation a vibrant
reality.

Some of the most pain-racked psalms come to this conclusion through a careful working-out of the experience
moment by moment. Jesus himself repeated the first line of
Psalm 22, which then proceeds on its dismal way:

My God, my God, why have you forsaken me?
Why are you so far from saving me,
so far from heeding my groans?

> My God, by day I cry to you, but there is no answer;
> in the night I cry with no respite.

The Psalmist goes on to contrast the divine assistance to his forefathers with the terrible state he now has to endure: a worm rather than a man, the source of heartless ridicule to all those around him who gloat over the impotence of his professed confidence in God to ameliorate his situation. He is surrounded by ferocious animals out to destroy him, while his strength drains away in despair. There are passages that foreshadow Christ's crucifixion:

> I tell my tale of misery,
> while they look on gloating.
> They share out my clothes among them
> and cast lots for my garments.

He prays once again for God's help, and then comes the miracle: rescue is afforded in the most desperate situation, and the Psalmist's tension can relax into a paean of thanksgiving:

> I shall declare your fame to my associates,
> praising you in the midst of the assembly . . .
> For he has not scorned him who is downtrodden,
> nor shrunk in loathing from his plight,
> nor hidden his face from him,
> but he has listened to his cry for help.
> You inspire my praise in the great assembly;
> I shall fulfil my vows in the sight of those who fear
>   you.

The psalm ends triumphantly with the thought that coming generations will be told of God's righteous deeds, and how he has acted decisively in the cause of justice.

The use of this psalm by Jesus on the cross raises the question as to whether he was pouring out his great pain or rehearsing God's final triumph. It seems probable that Jesus did feel bereft of his Father's presence, for the drama connected with this episode in the crucifixion speaks of something more desperate than a mere quoting of a psalm that ends on a note of triumph. The parallel accounts in Matthew 27:45–49 and Mark 15:33–39 are piercing in their agony that has no pleasant denouement in sight. Good Friday was a ghastly tragedy to all who looked on; but as we say in the Nicene Creed, 'On the third day he rose again in accordance with the Scriptures'. This is the miracle of God's grace that redeems our much less terrible travail, not so much by restoring that which was lost as by giving something completely new that alters our perspective of reality. In his own agony, the Psalmist penetrated the mystery of universal pain that is the presage of universal resurrection.

Another psalm that has Gospel affinities is Psalm 31 which starts with a confident appeal to the Lord:

> You are my rock and my stronghold;
> lead and guide me for the honour of your name.
> Set me free from the net that has been hidden to catch me;
> for you are my refuge.
> Into your hand I commit my spirit.
> You have delivered me, Lord, you God of truth.

The first five verses of this psalm, of which these lines are the end, are used in the office of compline; the penultimate verse was quoted by Jesus on the cross as the last of his 'seven words' (Luke 23:46), at least in the Church's tradition in relation to preaching the 'seven last words' on Good Friday.

Then comes a description of his present suffering: his misery has reduced his body to a state of wasting, his enemies scorn him while his neighbours find him a burden. Even his friends shudder and then pass by on the other side of the street as quickly as possible. Here one has visions of the Parable of the Good Samaritan where the priest and Levite pass by on the other side from the man who has been assaulted and robbed. Even more pertinent is the manner in which Jesus' disciples ran away when he was betrayed and showed his powerlessness, Peter denying so much as ever knowing him on three occasions.

Like the dead I have passed out of mind;
I have become like some article thrown away.
For I hear many
whispering threats from every side,
conspiring together against me
and scheming to take my life.

But the Psalmist puts his trust in God to rescue him from the
hands of his foes, a climax being reached in a passage of
imprecation against the wicked. And then comes relief; God
conceals the just under the protection of his presence, safe
from both conspirators and mischief-makers. The Lord is
blessed, and an answer is given to the first verse of Psalm 22:

In sudden alarm I said,
'I am shut out from your sight.'
But you heard my plea
when I called to you for help.

Then comes the final injunction to love God, who protects
the faithful but punishes the arrogant:

'Be strong and stout-hearted,
all you whose hope is in the Lord.'

The problem arises as to how one may be strong and stout-
hearted in a time of severe strain as described in this psalm.
It is somewhat reminiscent of telling a neurotically fearful
person to pull himself together; the advice may be sound but
no indication is provided as to how he should proceed. The
answer is one of pure faith; in the meantime God fills us with
such quiet strength that we are able to proceed in a mood of
confidence that owes little to external circumstances but much
to the Spirit of God within us. If our conscience is unclouded
we need fear no evil; if we know that we have sinned, we
have only to confess in open confidence to God for the
relationship to be restored and composure given to us. Our
consolation lies, paradoxically, in our own inability to solve
our difficulties, so that we need feel no guilt on this account.

But when we give ourselves in trust to God, resting in the Lord's love, we are given the strength to carry on even when the darkness shows no immediate sign of lifting. We are indeed saved by faith and not by our own works lest we should boast (Eph. 2:9) and thereby assume something of the divine power. In the end we may be able to enjoy the darkness as much as the light, inasmuch as we are illuminated by the inner light of God that neither flickers nor can be extinguished.

The secret is the practice of prayer, and its attainment is the final object of human life. Jesus himself said, 'the Son can do nothing by himself; he does only what he sees the Father doing: whatever the Father does, the Son does' (John 5:19). In the end, as we know, the Son had to do it all alone while the Father stood by, and by his victory over the darkness the Son is with us also when we traverse our own path of suffering. The Father does not intervene lest we should not gain the benefits of our own travail, but he has left a witness to accompany us and a promise of final achievement that will never fail.

A psalm of much greater joy comes later; in Psalm 107 the writer relates three different types of suffering and their joyful reversal by the love of God.

It is good to give thanks to the Lord,
for his love endures for ever.
So let them say who were redeemed by the Lord,
redeemed by him from the power of the enemy
and gathered out of the lands,
from east and west, from north and south.

First comes a recital of the travail of the Jews returning home from Babylonian exile, some lost in the desert wastes, hungry and desperate. But their cries to God were answered, and they were led to inhabited towns until they reached their destination. Then follows a more harrowing account of those who had brought pain upon themselves because of having flouted God's purposes and defied his commands. In their desolation they called for help, and the Lord saved them from

71

the darkness of imprisonment and the agony of despair. We indeed suffer in this way when we disregard the wisdom of God, as did Adam and Eve in their allegorical journey to self-understanding after they had repudiated the heaven in which they had been originally placed. But the divine assistance is never denied us provided we have the humility to seek it and the integrity to turn away from self-indulgence to obedience, from selfishness to service. The problem is always to keep up this declared conversion to the light and not slide back into the darkness; the entire Old Testament narrative is a development of this theme. In the New Testament the light is fully revealed, but, as we know only too well twenty centuries later, it is very hard to remain in its testing love.

Finally there is the celebrated account of God's help to those who sail the oceans:

> Others there are who go to sea in ships,
> plying their trade in the wide ocean.
> These have seen what the Lord has done,
> his marvellous actions in the deep.

The Psalmist describes the terror of the storm, the sailors being carried up to the skies and plunged down into the depths, and tossed to and fro in peril. One's mind immediately focuses on the story of Jonah and the sailors on the ship on which he tried to escape from doing this duty. Only when God's name was invoked and obedience sworn did the storm subside; the innocent sailors resumed the work and Jonah was ready to preach repentance to the Ninevites. And so, in the psalm, the seamen's cries bring them out of trouble as the storm subsides, and God guides them to the harbour that was their destination. Then they praise the Lord for his enduring love and his marvellous works.

The fulfilment of the storm episode in the story of Jonah and Psalm 107 is the presence of Jesus himself in the storm-buffeted ship of Matthew 8:23–27. With God the Son among the crew an inner power is shown that can still the waves, but, like Jonah, the Lord has first to be awakened. God may start his work from outside, but in the end the power is to be given to those who follow him.

To return to Psalm 46:10, when we can let be and learn of the divine presence, that presence infuses our own being and fills us with power beyond our simple understanding. The greatest power is courage to face the immediate present with strength and purpose.

The psalm attains its climax with a recital of God's many wonderful works so that the righteous may prosper, while tyrants, for all their worldly power, are brought into misfortune and sorrow. This theme of the Wisdom literature deserves closer inspection, for life is not always as clear-cut as this, but we can reiterate the Psalmist's enthusiasm for God's righteousness:

> Let them give thanks to the Lord for his enduring love
> and for the marvellous things he has done for mankind.
> Let them exalt him in the assembly of the people
> and praise him in the elders' council.

The beautiful Psalm 84 gives some indication of the rewards of suffering. It is a pilgrimage hymn for those on their way to Jerusalem whose end is the Temple itself.

> Lord of Hosts,
> how dearly loved is your dwelling-place!
> I pine and faint with longing
> for the courts of the Lord's temple;
> my whole being cries out with joy
> to the living God.

Like the birds of the air the pilgrim has found his home in the Temple, not of course as a place of residence but as a habitation of eternal rest. Here there is ceaseless praise, not merely with words that flow from the lips but with an open heart pouring out God's blessings to the world.

The sixth verse is especially important:

As they pass through the waterless valley
the Lord fills it with springs,
and the early rain covers it with pools.

So much of our life is arid and unproductive, our enforced
journey a drudgery rather than any apparent pilgrimage. We
look for a change of fortune as if we deserved it, as if it should
be ours by right, but in fact our eyes are so concentrated on
our own condition that we fail to take full account of the
greater world around us. We long for a change while we are
oblivious of the potential glory in our very midst and within
our seeking grasp; if only we would awaken from our self-
centred slumber and participate wholeheartedly in the events
of the present moment.

If we see life as a pilgrimage, our sufferings become pro-
ductive; the desert blossoms with new life, and every moment
reveals a prodigy of God's glory. The pilgrim has his eyes
fixed on his destination; his creature comforts cease to
impinge on his consciousness as a primary concern, and yet,
not surprisingly, they are satisfied. The law enunciated in
Matthew 6:33 is fully proved, 'Set your mind on God's kingdom and his justice before everything else, and all the rest
will come to you as well.' The person who sees life as a
pilgrimage will never be disappointed; his fellow who looks
for personal advantages will be miserable even if many
material assets come his way. The explanation is that his eyes
are so set on the barely attainable, and the jealousy that
comes with it, that the splendour of the present moment
passes him ludicrously by. In the words of St Paul, 'In our
sorrows we have always cause for joy; poor ourselves, we
bring wealth to many; penniless, we own the world' (2 Cor.
6:10).

The Psalmist prays for the anointed one, probably either
king or high priest depending on when the psalm was composed in relation to the Babylonian exile, and then follows
the famous verse:

Better one day in your courts
than a thousand days in my home;

74

better to linger by the threshold of God's house
than to live in the dwellings of the wicked.

To know God with that unselfconscious intimacy is the goal
of our life. In him alone is the rest which we all seek, a rest
that strengthens us effortlessly for the work ahead, which we
can anticipate and greet with enthusiasm. The writer is thinking of the magnificent Temple, but this is merely the outer
form of the heavenly design shown to Moses on Mount Sinai,
and revealed to us also in our own lives as we enter the silence
of dedication to God, and by extension to our fellow creatures
also. Indeed, in the splendid vision of the new Jerusalem that
comes near the end of the Book of Revelation, there is no
Temple, for its Temple is the sovereign Lord God and the
Lamb (21:22). While we live on earth it is right that we
should work towards earthly ideals, but if these are spiritually
based and not merely objects of personal aggrandisement,
they lead us past themselves to the life of eternity. In other
words the things of this world that are treated with reverence
assume the nature of sacraments, no matter how far the
person may be from spiritual knowledge. The vibrant heart
has its own tacit understanding, an understanding so common
in the psalms, but so easily overlooked by the casual reader.

And so comes the final affirmation of God's glory and his
love:

The Lord God is a sun and shield;
grace and honour are his to bestow.
The Lord withholds no good thing
from those whose life is blameless.
O Lord of Hosts,
happy are they who trust in you!

It is nevertheless right to end this chapter on a more solemn
note. In earthly life our suffering is seldom removed as by a
miracle; instead we have to learn to bear it, hoping ultimately
to grow through it. Psalm 90, a favourite of mine, sees the
human condition in calm, sombre perspective.

> Lord, you have been our refuge
> throughout all generations.
> Before the mountains were brought forth
> or the earth and the world were born,
> from age to age you are God.

God has complete power in his universe, being able to turn his people back to dust, for in his sight a thousand years are as the passing of one day. Rather in the manner of the very different Psalm 103, the writer laments the frailty of the human condition:

> You cut them off;
> they are asleep in death.
> They are like grass which shoots up;
> though in the morning it flourishes and shoots up,
> by evening it droops and withers.

The writer sees the human condition as being perpetually under God's judgement; all our days pass under the divine wrath because of our sins. Even if we attain the customary seventy or eighty years, our lives are but toil and sorrow. The Psalmist speaks much of the divine wrath which punishes us unremittingly for our offences, but a more helpful way of assessing the situation is to relate wrath to law; one cannot infringe any moral law, including that of the state, without incurring the prescribed punishment. This 'wrath' of the Creator is a measure of the love he feels for us: nothing but its best will suffice. 'My son, do not spurn the Lord's correction or recoil from his reproof; for those whom the Lord loves he reproves, and he punishes the son who is dear to him' (Prov. 3:11–12).

When we come to our senses, we can see the prospect ahead of us, an insignificant period of strength followed by a void of helplessness:

> So make us know how few are our days,
> that our minds may learn wisdom.

This is the supreme reward of suffering, greater even than the marvellous relief and reversal of fortune so often encountered in the psalms and rather less dramatically but equally joyously in our own lives. The chastened Psalmist yearns for a demonstration of God's love and power, so that there may be days of gladness for those of the previous humiliation, not only personal but also national. But until wisdom has been acquired, all God's bounty will be wasted.

> May the favour of the Lord our God be on us,
> Establish for us all that we do,
> establish it firmly.

So ends this darkly-tinted, but hopeful, psalm. The successful undertakings that the Psalmist requests can only be realized with some degree of permanence when the people can cooperate intelligently and resolutely with the divine assistance. Wisdom has to take the place of indulgent folly. To depend on God reversing an unpleasant situation is childishness; to offer oneself as a child in the service of God is the way of wisdom. Childlikeness includes a humility that will learn from every circumstance; it is an attitude essential for the acquisition of true wisdom.

9

The Penitent Heart

The close communion that the Psalmist has with God is movingly sincere. Not only are the dark emotions shared so that their psychic charge can be released and given to God, who directs them towards understanding instead of fruitless revolt, but the constant undercurrent of guilt is also unashamedly laid bare. Guilt is the inner fruit of sin, which is most constructively seen as a failure to live up to our full potentiality, to have missed the mark set before us. We all have a spark of God within us, the inner light, and anything done which clouds that light casts its shadow of guilt in the deep recesses of the soul. In the wonderful prologue of the Fourth Gospel the writer considers the Son of God in three modalities. Firstly he is the Word whereby creation is effected by the Father. Secondly he is the life which is the light of mankind (the inner light). And thirdly he is the incarnate Lord who came into the world and to his own people as Jesus of Nazareth. All who accepted him were given the right to become children of God. And so the Word became flesh; he made his home among his people Israel, and in due course the three disciples Peter, James and John were privileged to witness his transfiguration, the glory such as befits the Father's only Son, full of grace and truth (John 1:1–14).

There is therefore an inseparable link between the human soul and the Word. There is an immense spiritual future for us all, and when we betray this deep calling the soul is scorched in its confrontation with the searing truth of God. This is made known as the inner light and also the tradition that we have inherited; this is the Law, brought up to date, as it were, for the present time. While its truth can never

change, it is, like everything else, being constantly renewed
by the power of the Holy Spirit. 'The written law condemns
to death, but the Spirit gives life' (2 Cor. 3:6).

Psalm 36 confronts the condition of sinfulness very starkly:

A wicked person's talk is prompted by sin in his heart;
he sees no need to fear God.
For it flatters and deceives him
and, when his iniquity is found out, he does not
    change.

He is a liar, his conduct is vicious, and the course of his life
a criminal one.

Then comes the contrast of God's righteousness:

Lord, your unfailing love reaches to the heavens,
your faithfulness to the skies.
Your righteousness is like the lofty mountains,
your justice like the great deep . . .
for with you is the fountain of life,
and by your light we are enlightened.

The psalm concludes with a prayer for God's continuing love
and saving power for those who know him, namely the honest
of heart, against the snares of the wicked. In the end it is the
evildoers who are cast down and unable to rise.

Nevertheless there can be few of us who at some time in
our lives have not been among the ranks of the unrighteous.
This applies as much to those in ecclesiastical and political
authority as to the less auspicious people that throng the
streets. And so there are a number of frankly penitential
psalms for those who repent of their past misdemeanours.
Traditionally these are Psalms 6, 32, 38, 51, 102, 130 and
143.

Psalm 6 is one spoken in the ordeal of sickness:

Lord, do not rebuke me in your anger,
do not punish me in your wrath.

> Show favour to me, Lord, for my strength fails;
> Lord, heal me, for my body is racked with pain.

The writer goes on to describe the magnitude of his suffering, praying to be spared from death, for among the dead no one remembers God, nor can praise come from Sheol. He then calls for relief from his adversaries, workers of evil who probably gloat over his distress, which they can smugly ascribe to just punishment for some sin of the past. The psalm ends with an assurance of divine acceptance and the promise of victory over the forces of darkness.

The theme of enemies gloating over the Psalmist's travail is prominent also in Psalm 41, itself not numbered amongst the penitential set:

> 'His case is desperate,' my enemies say;
> 'when will he die and his name perish?'
> All who visit me speak from hearts devoid of sincerity;
> they are keen to gather bad news
> and go out to spread it abroad . . .
> Even the friend whom I trusted, who ate at my table,
> exults over my misfortune.

This verse brings us to the work of Judas Iscariot at the Last Supper, but should also point a finger at our own insincerity when an acquaintance is ill. How often are we outwardly shocked while inwardly exultant at the downfall of someone of merit? The news helps to avert our gaze from our own infirmity. It also satisfies our jealousy. The matter is further considered on page 44 in relation to Psalm 55.

Psalm 32 strikes a happier note:

> Happy is he whose offence is forgiven,
> whose sin is blotted out!

While the Psalmist remained intransigent his body lay wasting away, but once he had acknowledged his faults, confessing them frankly to God, the penalty of his sin was remitted. And so the writer can exult in the strength and compassion of his

Creator, encouraging his fellows to renounce their obstinacy
and likewise make their peace with God:

> Many are the torments for the ungodly,
> but unfailing love enfolds those who trust in the Lord.
> Rejoice in the Lord and be glad, you righteous ones;
> sing aloud, all you of honest heart.

Psalm 38 is very similar in tone and content to Psalm 6,
but the intensity of suffering is greatly magnified:

> My wounds fester and stink because of my folly.
> I am bowed down and utterly prostrate.
> All day long I go about as if in mourning,
> for my loins burn with fever,
> and there is no wholesome flesh in me.
> Faint and badly crushed
> I groan aloud in anguish of heart.

The realism of this account of disease is so stark that one
wonders whether the writer had not contracted some infec-
tious ailment, possibly a sexually transmitted one, as a result
of his folly. Certainly the account is relevant to the current
situation of venereal diseases even if the condition described
was quite different. The pattern of disease may change, but
its underlying cause, unwholesome living, remains. And, lest
we feel virtuously superior to the victim of such a condition,
let us remember that no one is exempt from its ravages, so
closely knit is human society. We do indeed belong to one
another as parts of one body (Eph. 4:25). This well-known
observation was made by St Paul in respect of the young
Christian community, but now it is of obvious universal application.

> My friends and companions shun me in my sickness,
> and my kinsfolk keep far off . . .
> But I am like a deaf man, hearing nothing,
> like a dumb man who cannot open his mouth . . .

81

> I make no secret of my iniquity;
> I am troubled because of my sin.

Once again there is a complaint about the malice of his enemies, and the psalm ends with an urgent plea for divine aid.

The most powerful of the seven is Psalm 51; it is also by far the best known. Traditionally it is ascribed to King David, after his seduction of Bathsheba and cunning murder of her husband Uriah the Hittite was condemned by the prophet Nathan (2 Sam. 12:1–14). In fact it is of universal application in respect of callous betrayal and mean deceit such as few of us escape committing at some time in our lives.

The Psalmist throws himself unconditionally on the divine mercy, asking to be cleansed from his sins. He knows that it is, in fact, only against God that he has sinned, for he has tarnished the divine image in which he was created. This iniquity is more fundamental than any harm he may have done a fellow creature:

> From my birth I have been evil,
> sinful from the time my mother conceived me.

This is a basic statement of the human condition. We need not believe in 'original sin' as something we inherited from our allegorical first ancestor Adam, following the tragedy of the Fall. It is more satisfactory, and certainly more scientifically based, to see a fundamental imperfection in everything God has made. This does not necessarily deny the goodness of the divine creation so much as affirm its opportunity for development into full identity. In each of us there are two principles at work: self-interest and higher concern for others. Without the first we should not survive very long in our hard world, but without the second we would become mere power-intoxicated people at enmity with all our fellows as we strove against them for survival and mastery. The end would be a war of attrition.

Experience brings enlightenment with it, and we begin to see that the great fruit of survival is the service we can provide others; as we serve without self-interest, so real happiness pours through us. Looking forward to nothing, we can begin to live in eternity, and this is the supreme gift of God to a rational creature like the human being. It is thus that the sinful impulse lamented by the Psalmist is overcome and the personality strengthened for service on a universal level. St Paul rightly sees God alone as being able to deliver us from the divided consciousness of worldly life, where we act contrary to the deepest intuition within us, to the unitary consciousness of Christ (Rom. 7:25).

> God, create a pure heart for me,
> and give me a new and steadfast spirit.
> Do not drive me from your presence
> or take your holy spirit from me.

The Psalmist craves for a renewal of the previous right relationship with God by an act of free justification by God. Then the spirit within, which is the 'point' of the soul where moral and spiritual values are apprehended, can emerge clean and radiant.

> Lord, open my lips,
> that my mouth may proclaim your praise.
> You have no delight in sacrifice;
> if I were to bring a whole-offering you would not accept
>   it.
> God, my sacrifice is a broken spirit;
> you, God, will not despise a chastened heart.

Here is another great truth: our most valuable sacrifice is not of objects but of ourselves. The story of the widow's mite in Mark 12:41–44 amplifies this truth. But the Psalmist's sacrifice, unlike even that of the impoverished widow who at least gave some money, is contemptible by human standards – merely a broken personality. But this is as acceptable to God as are wonderful spiritual feats or material excellence: the Parable of the Publican and the Pharisee once more gives us the right perspective. Whatever is faced squarely and given to God with reverence, no matter how unpleasant it may appear, can be transformed by the divine grace so that a new creature emerges. Whatever we take special pride over can easily serve to separate us from our fellows and also from God. We all have to learn the lesson of sharing ourselves with others.

The psalm ends on a national note, perhaps added later: there is a prayer for Zion's prosperity and the walls of Jerusalem (rebuilt under Nehemiah after the return from Babylonian exile). Even animal sacrifice will be acceptable, now offered with devotion instead of mechanical rectitude. We would not at the present time consider offering animal sacrifices, but there could be something of our own treasury that might be given to God's service. Whatever impoverishes us, no matter how small it might appear in the world's eyes, seems to be of great value to God.

The psalm shows very clearly where joy is to be found: in a right relationship with God and our fellow creatures. Any action that transgresses this law puts us out of fellowship with humans and out of saving health with God. But all we have to do is to move beyond pride, confess our sins, await absolution, and then by an act of undivided will follow the path that is set before us: 'There must be no limit to your goodness, as your heavenly Father's goodness knows no bounds' (Matt. 5:48). It is not the work we have to do that matters; it is the manner in which we do the work that is the basis of the judgement set before us.

Psalm 102 repeats the well-remembered themes of penitence: the personal affliction of the sinner, his isolation, and the savage taunts of his enemies. But then follows a cry for help for Zion, which has been destroyed presumably by the Babylonian invaders. Clearly there is a connection between the sin of the individual and the humiliation of the community with its destroyed country. Even the wickedness of a single person has repercussions far outside his limited social presence, so closely are we all parts of the one body of our community. But the divine presence outlasts all human folly, and can be relied on for restoration once we have come to our senses:

Long ago you laid earth's foundations,
and the heavens were your handiwork.
They will all pass away, but you remain;
like clothes they will all wear out . . .
But you are the same and your years will have no end.

Psalm 130 is the shortest and loveliest of the penitential group. It is one of the Songs of the Ascents sung by pilgrims on the way to Jerusalem, mentioned on page 24. The Psalmist has called to God out of the depths of his suffering, the result of past sins, and prays for the Lord's attention; if God should keep account of sins who could survive? But God's nature is one of mercy and forgiveness, and this clemency leads us to revere our Creator even more than his strength fills us with fear and foreboding.

Let Israel look for the Lord.
For in the Lord is love unfailing,
and great is his power to deliver.
He alone will set Israel free
from all their sins.

The psalm is thus not merely one of penitence but also of hope. It is frequently recited at funeral services (others often used are Psalms 23, 90 and 121 as well as passages from Psalms 27, 42, 118 and 139).

I wait for the Lord with longing;
I put my hope in his word.
My soul waits for the Lord
more eagerly than watchmen for the morning.

When we die, we will have to face the results of the life we lived while in the protection of the physical body. The pain that may follow the full realization of our past life is taken up by God as soon as we ask for help. This is a very real application of Jesus' promise, 'Ask, and you will receive; seek, and you will find; knock, and the door will be opened to you. For everyone who asks receives, those who seek find, and to those who knock, the door will be opened' (Matt. 7:7–8). What we are given is not a miraculous removal of a past problem but an accession of strength that helps us to cope with the matter and work towards its solution. Once we are in proper relationship with God, a circumstance which always follows an honest act of contrition, he is with us, and, in the words of Psalm 23, 'his shepherd's staff and crook afford us comfort'. And so the mourner may move from dark lamentation to radiant hope; to be sure, the mood will not last indefinitely, but as we repeat the psalm, we may remember the writer's own experience and his final victory, one sufficient to have allowed him to sing to God in hope for future trials. And he sings it on his pilgrimage to Jerusalem, an allegory of our eternal pilgrimage to God's heavenly city.

As St Paul writes in 2 Corinthians 4:17 to 5:2:

Our troubles are slight and short-lived, and their outcome is an eternal glory which far outweighs them, provided our eyes are fixed, not on the things that are seen, but on the things that are unseen; for what is seen is transient, what is unseen is eternal. We know that if the earthly frame that houses us today is demolished, we possess a building which God has provided, a house not made by human hands, eternal and in heaven.

Psalm 143 is the final one of the set of seven. It follows the more usual pattern of praying to God, acknowledging that no person is innocent before him. The writer has been sorely crushed by an enemy and left to lie in darkness like a corpse. In his dire distress he remembers God's past providence, praying for a similar favour now in the time of trial. Like Psalm 119, but in much shorter compass, there is a request that God instruct him how to follow his will and show him the way he should take, for his heart is set on the Lord. One suspects that this conversion to the light is the fruit of the Psalmist's distress, and can only hope the change in heart is not merely makeshift, as in the parody of a penitential prayer composed in Hosea 6:1–3. How easy it is to cry out for help when we are in agony, promising all kinds of amendments of our previous lifestyle when we are well again! How much easier it is to forget it all when we are cured! The healing of the ten lepers described in Luke 17:11–19 is a case in point: they all cried aloud to Jesus for help, and all were cured of the skin disease that had caused them so much embarrassment, but only one, a despised foreigner, came back to give thanks.

> Revive me, Lord, for the honour of your name:
> be my deliverer; release me from distress.

There is finally a common note of vengeance against the writer's enemies, whom he would gladly see exterminated, for he is God's servant. We have considered the problem of the conflicting demands of justice and love on page 42. In the psalms justice is emphasized. It is only when we attain a greater degree of self-knowledge that we cease to be merely judgemental, but in addition offer a helping hand to the transgressor as a prelude to his own conversion to the light.

A psalm that typifies the attitude of the impenitent is Psalm 14, with its nearly identical counterpart, Psalm 53. In the first the divine name Yahweh, revealed to Moses, is used, whereas Psalm 53 uses Elohim, the common noun for God.

> The impious fool says in his heart,
> 'There is no God.'
> Everyone is depraved, every deed is vile;
> no one does good!

The fool is probably not so much a dogmatic atheist as one who acts as if God paid no attention to human actions, either through remoteness or sheer apathy. If a person does not remember God in his heart, his actions will tend to foster corruption and cause general confusion. Without God our actions lack a guiding wisdom and will tend to be determined by the exigencies of the present moment, irrespective of later consequences.

Have they no understanding,
all these evildoers who devour my people as if eating
    bread,
and never call to the Lord?

The godless person is very liable to revert insidiously to evil ways once he moves beyond the guidance of his parents and mentors. The exercise of power and sharp practices brings in a more rapid reward; it is only later that their bad effects fall back on the agent as well as his victims. In the version of Psalm 53, which is rather more trustworthy than Psalm 14 at this point:

They will be in dire alarm
when God scatters the bones of the godless,
confounded when God rejects them.

It needs to be said that the bones of the godless are heedlessly scattered because of their own previously thoughtless lifestyle and not by a vindictive God who demands obedience in order to demonstrate his authority. We can easily reject God and live selfish, destructive lives oblivious of his presence, but God will never cast us aside; his nature is pure love, but he cannot interfere until we acknowledge the folly of our ways and call to him for help in sincere prayer, guided by chastened humility.

Psalm 12 is another brief essay on this theme: the writer calls on God's help because no one who is loyal remains. There is no good faith, and all conversation is corrupted by lies and duplicity in the guise of charm and reassurance. The words of these hypocrites are deceitful, but God will see justice done to the poor and plundered.

Unlike the subtle language of the unjust, impenitent sinner:

The words of the Lord are unalloyed:
silver refined in a crucible,
gold purified seven times over.
Lord, you are our protector
and will for ever guard us from such people.

But meanwhile, alas, the wicked parade about, and worthless things are most highly prized. Psalm 12 is a perpetually topical commentary on the state of a secular society. Conscience can so easily be disregarded as the end tends to justify the means. But, to be honest, the same situation has often reared its head in the midst of a vigorous theocracy. The practice of a religion can as easily divert one's attention from the deeper realities as focus it upon them. It is probable that more cruelty has been committed in the name of God than for any other cause. The god of religion may have to be discarded before the Living God can make his home with us in the depth of our soul.

10

Of Times and Seasons

The sun rises and the sun goes down; then it speeds to its place and rises there again. The wind blows to the south, it veers to the north; round and round it goes and returns full circle. All streams run into the sea, yet the sea never overflows; back to the place from which the streams ran they return to run again.

So runs the discouraging comment on life in Ecclesiastes 1:5–7. The wearisome vanity of life that the Speaker of this Wisdom book describes is in fact more a comment on his own mental state than the perpetual flux of the natural order. To some people the skies are merely dark accumulations of sunless clouds, but others soon see the glory of sunrise and the beauty of a slowly fading sunset. The Psalmist belongs to the second category, as we have already noted in relation to Psalm 104, where the wonder of nature, God's great creation, is celebrated.

If we cannot see God's presence in the things around us, we will not find it in philosophical speculation or theological debate. As St Paul says in Romans 1:19–20, all that can be known of God lies plain before our eyes; indeed God himself has disclosed it to us. Ever since the world began, his invisible attributes, that is to say his everlasting power and Deity, have been visible to the eye of reason in the things he has made. While we must not identify the Creator with his creation, we can certainly see his mind in his works and his love in allowing his creatures to follow their own choice, while always being available when called upon in prayer.

We live in a world limited by time and space; it is the first

of these that interests us in this chapter. There is first of all
the unending procession of the hours of the day. Morning is
celebrated in Psalms 3 and 5. It is the time of God's favour;
certainly we awake refreshed at this time of the day, for a
good period of sleep seems to clear away the emotional debris
of the past hours. It is at this time, preferably shortly after
rising, that prayer is especially keen, since our minds are open
and alive rather than closed with worry and tired with strain
as they may be later on. And so we can offer ourselves to
God for his service as we start a new day's work.

Psalm 3 describes a familiar situation: the writer's enemies
are set against him, but he calls on the Lord for help:

> I lie down and sleep,
> and I awake again, for the Lord upholds me.
> I shall not fear their myriad forces
> ranged against me on every side.

This verse reminds us of Jesus' resurrection and by extension
our own growth in sanctity through travail and heavenly rest.
The Psalmist calls on God to save him while destroying his
enemies. Such is the Lord's victory, while his people are
blessed at the same time.

Psalm 5 pursues the same theme of petition and imprecation against the arrogant and those who practise wickedness.

> When I pray to you, Lord,
> in the morning you will hear me.
> I shall prepare a morning sacrifice
> and keep watch.

There is the common oscillating pattern of praying for help,
praise for God's justice, denunciation of the enemy, and a
confident expectation of the divine help:

> For you, Lord, will bless the righteous;
> you will surround them with favour as with a shield.

91

Psalms 4 and 134 celebrate evening, a time traditionally of trial and suffering. Both are said at the office of compline. Psalm 4 once again calls on the divine assistance in the face of attacks by enemies. These bow down to empty idols and false gods; they should learn that God has singled out for himself his loyal servant, who hears when his devoted follower calls.

> Let awe restrain you from sin;
> while you rest, meditate in silence:
> Offer your due of sacrifice,
> and put your trust in the Lord.

While many people yearn for material prosperity, the Psalmist knows greater happiness from God's presence in his life than others would from all their grain and wine. The psalm ends with the lovely thought:

> Now in peace I shall lie down and sleep;
> for it is you alone, Lord, who let me live in safety.

The delightful little Psalm 134 ends the series of Songs of the Ascents. It is a hymn of blessing for all God's servants, those who minister night after night in the Temple.

> Lift up your hands towards the sanctuary
> and bless the Lord.
> May the Lord, maker of heaven and earth,
> bless you from Zion!

Verses from these two evening psalms form an excellent theme for quiet meditation just before going to bed; another useful focus of meditation is the Nunc Dimittis spoken by the devout Simeon when the infant Jesus was presented in the Temple (Luke 2:29–32). They lift up the mind from the slough of material worry and emotional tension to a realm where the peace of God is knowable. In the end we receive according to our physical capacity no less than God's prodigality towards us. Beautiful psalms, like fine music, cleanse the organs of perception and the brain which receives all incoming information. Thus we are able to sleep better as we commend ourselves in this wonderful flow of words to God's grace. And in that sleep many wonderful ideas are being incorporated into a living philosophy.

Psalm 67 remembers the time of harvest. It begins with a prayer for God's continued beneficence:

> May God be gracious to us and bless us,
> may he cause his face to shine on us.

Then his purpose, his saving power among the nations, will be widely known. He will be praised by all the peoples as a judge of equity and a loving guide to all the nations. The universal hope, that all people will be received into the Holy City of God, seldom receives more generous articulation than here. The promise of this is to be seen in what has already been given:

> The earth has yielded its harvest.
> May God, our God, bless us.
> God grant us his blessing,
> that all the ends of the earth may fear him.

It cannot be emphasized too often that the fear which the Lord requires is not a shaking in its boots of a terrified population but an acknowledgement of God's sovereignty, or holiness, and a serious commitment to lead a life of holiness in response to the divine initiative. The Ten Commandments show us the way of such a life, and the practice of constant prayer opens us to the love of God which alone can make that way a possible venture. As Jesus says, 'What is impossible for men is possible for God' (Luke 18:27).

The much more sombre Psalm 39, which shares a mood of acceptance and wisdom with Psalm 90, considers the short span of human life in comparison with God's eternity. The Psalmist vows a perfectly sinless life, keeping silent in the face of his enemy. The silence penetrates to the very depth of his being, and then a more sober appraisal of his situation causes him to speak with wisdom:

> Lord, let me know my end and the number of my days;
> tell me how short my life is to be.
> I know you have made my days a mere span long,
> and my whole life is as nothing in your sight.
> A human being, however firm he stands, is but a puff
> of wind.

As the writer of Ecclesiastes would have agreed, the strength of worldly wealth is a mere illusion; no one knows who finally will enjoy it. And so the Psalmist throws himself upon the divine mercy:

> Now, Lord, what do I wait for?
> My hope is in you.
> Deliver me from all who do me wrong;
> make me no longer the butt of fools.

The writer sees God as his punishing agent, but in fact it is the law of life, enshrined in the Law given to Moses on Mount Sinai, that is the arbiter. There is no escape from the fundamental law of cause and effect, but once we are secure in God's love and are on the true way of life that leads to holiness, every effect, no matter how fearful it may appear, is invested with such hope that the understanding it brings with it is seen to be a blessing and not a curse. This is the supreme fruit of suffering, that we may bring compassion to others:

> Frown on me no more; let me look cheerful
> before I depart and cease to be.

Psalm 71 deals more specifically with the time of old age. The writer here has always been loyal to God, though his sufferings have made him like a portent to those around him who cannot equate pain with goodness. Nevertheless the Psalmist's praise to God will not falter nor his witness of the divine truth. However, like all of us, the future presents an unknown quantity, and our faith is stretched as we contemplate the wasteland of the aged:

> Do not cast me off when old age comes
> or forsake me as my strength fails,
> for my enemies whisper against me
> and those who spy on me intrigue together.

Once again the writer declares his trust in God. He remembers his staunch faith in the past which issued forth in good works. But then once more comes the fear of the future:

> Now that I am old and my hair is grey,
> do not forsake me, God,
> until I have extolled your strength
> to generations yet to come,
> your might and vindicating power to highest heaven;
> for great are the things you have done.
> Who is there like you, my God?

The oscillating moods of faith, triumph and doubt that are so common in the psalms generally, are seen here with particularly great poignancy. Weakness cuts us all down to size, and old age is seldom a pleasant experience, as the physical body's functions fail and we depend more and more on the solicitude of others. The Jews have for generations had strong family loyalty, so that their aged folk are well provided for either at home or in desirable communal situations where their spiritual health is cared for no less than their bodily comforts. But most of us have no such caring people to trust. Parents all too often become a burden on their children, not infrequently because of their own psychological difficulties that are not ameliorated with the passage of time. We do indeed create our own old age when we are still young. The wise person lives so compassionately while he is fit that when he too needs help his attitude evokes spontaneous love from those who tend him. One hopes this was the case of the writer of Psalm 71.

This is a very practical fruit of good living: 'Always treat others as you would like them to treat you: this is the law and the prophets' (Matt. 7:12). The advice of Ecclesiastes 12:1 is equally pertinent, 'Remember your Creator in the days of your youth, before the bad times come and the years draw near when you will say "I have no pleasure in them".' The chapter proceeds with a very realistic description of old age and death without any comfort of survival of the personality to soften it. Faith illuminated by inner experience helps to broaden the picture.

A much more pleasant occasion is celebrated in Psalm 45, the marriage between a king and his chosen princess, though both Jewish and Christian tradition see it in Messianic terms: the union of the Messiah with Israel, or with his Church in the Christian tradition. In fact the two interpretations are not mutually exclusive, for a true marriage between a devoted couple is a sacrament of God's love for his creation. And where there is reciprocated love, there is also a witness of resurrection. As we read in the Song of Songs 8:6 and 7, love is strong as death, and many waters cannot quench love, no flood can sweep it away; if someone were to offer for love all the wealth in his house, it would be laughed to scorn.

The Messianic king is fulsomely praised:

> You surpass all others in beauty;
> gracious words flow from your lips,
> for you are blessed by God for ever . . .
> God has enthroned you for all eternity;
> your royal sceptre is a sceptre of equity.

He has been anointed by God because he loves right and hates all that is wrong. His robes are fragrant with myrrh and powdered aloes, he is made glad by music, and princesses accompany him as his consort takes her place at his right hand. She is then told to follow her new way of life with diligence:

> Listen, my daughter, hear my words
> and consider them:

forget your own people and your father's house;
let the king desire your beauty,
for he is your lord.

She must enter a new way of life, of splendour, revelry and
rejoicing, as she assumes her place in the king's palace. Her
reward will be sons to succeed her forefathers, and they will
be made princes throughout the land.

I shall declare your fame through all generations;
therefore nations will praise you for ever and ever.

The injunction to the princess about forgetting her past life
reminds us of Abraham, the first clearly Israelite patriarch,
who was told by God to leave all the comfort and established
security of Mesopotamia and set out with his family to an
unknown country which would be shown to him. And so, at
the age of seventy-five he commenced a new life in Canaan
where remarkable adventures were to follow. It is thus also
with those who put their trust in the Lord and follow his
instructions in pure faith illuminated by honest endeavour.
A marriage has something of this nature as well; of course
the parents of the newly-wed couple are not forgotten in spirit,
but it is essential that both marriage partners should face
the future with courageous determination, and not look back
nostalgically on the past when they were free and uncommitted. It is indeed this matter of commitment that dis-
tinguishes a marriage from a mere liaison which can be ter-
minated at any time. Jesus says, 'No one who sets his hand
to the plough and then looks back is fit for the kingdom of
God' (Luke 9:62). The fruits of a marriage are maturity and
compassion; as one begins to see the less pleasant aspects of
one's own personality in the stress of a new relationship, so
one can be more open to God's undemanding love in one's
state of humiliation. The love of God accepts us as we are,
and the experience of this helps us to accept the other person
in his or her own right, and to cease making impossible
demands on him or her. In the royal marriage celebrated in
Psalm 45 we can envisage the slow growth in the personalities

of both partners; even the Messiah has to grow for the great work ahead of him.

Times past form the basis of history, and a number of psalms have deeply historical roots. Psalm 132, another one of the Songs of the Ascents, commemorates the translation of the Ark from the region of Jaar, which, like Bethlehem, Jesus' birthplace, was in the district of Ephrathah. It was to be carried to Jerusalem, there to be set up in a humble tent in the Citadel of David, which is Zion. Zion was the holy hill of Jerusalem, the very centre around which the hope of the whole nation revolved. King David reflected on the lowly situation of the Ark of the Covenant while he lived in splendour. He confided his concern to the prophet Nathan, who was told by God that a royal son would build the Temple to house the Ark, but that David himself was not eligible for the task. There followed the prophecy of Nathan concerning the future of the Davidic dynasty: so long as the ruler followed the way set down in the Law of Moses, all would be well. Any apostasy, however, would reverse the country's good fortune, until such a time as a new beneficent ruler emerged. The formula, 'I shall be a father to him, and he will be my son' (2 Sam. 7:14), was to characterize the relationship between God and his people Israel. We remember the teaching of Proverbs 3:11–12, 'My son, do not spurn the Lord's correction or recoil from his reproof; for those whom the Lord loves he reproves, and he punishes the son who is dear to him.' The historical context of Psalm 132 is found in 2 Samuel 6–7.

> Lord, remember David
> and all the adversity he endured;
> how he swore an oath to the Lord
> and made this vow to the Mighty One of Jacob:
> 'I will not live in my house
> nor will I go to my bed,
> I will give myself no rest,
> nor allow myself sleep,
> until I find a sanctuary for the Lord,
> a dwelling for the Mighty One of Jacob.'

This resolution is applicable to us also as we follow the call God has given us. To be sure, it may be far less auspicious than that of David, for most of us are destined to lead rather prosaic lives, but it is how we play our part that matters. Indeed usually our own contribution may apparently disappear in the mists of a not too spectacular family history, but later on a distinguished descendant may be born to carry out some important work. The many detailed genealogies that punctuate the scriptural record, including St Matthew's account of Jesus' ancestors (Matt. 1:1–17), emphasize this point. They all played their part in the history of salvation by simply 'being fruitful and increasing in numbers', as we considered on page 27.

> For the Lord has chosen Zion,
> desired her for his home . . .
> There I shall make a king of David's line appear
> and prepare a lamp for my anointed one;
> I shall cover his enemies with shame,
> but on him there will be a shining crown.

Psalms 68, 78, 89 and 105 also have strong historical roots. Psalm 68 is a triumphant account of Israelite history from the time of the exodus from Egypt up to the universal period when all the nations will come to worship the one God in Israel. Psalm 78 strikes a more sober note as it surveys the history of the Israelites during their long exodus and the early period in Canaan when the Judges ruled a recalcitrant people. Their frequent apostasies were the cause of their continual suffering until the triumphant reign of King David, which represents the highest point in early Israelite history. The psalm does not consider David's brilliant but unstable son Solomon, under whose rule the Temple was built and the nation split in two because of his infidelity to God. We have considered this theme on page 36. How easy it is to worship God unworthily under an imposing façade of religious ritual! Soon formal worship becomes something of an insurance policy against the time of trial, but, unlike the worldly policy, it brings no benefits with its claims. Only holy living can insure us against the day of disaster, because then alone is God's presence a real strength, as we remember from the first verse of Psalm 46.

We have considered Psalm 89 on page 46; like Psalm 132 it concentrates on God's promise made by Nathan to King David, but near the end there is the utter tragedy of an apparent failure of the divine love and faithfulness, two qualities that are often juxtaposed in the psalms, but never more movingly than in Psalm 89.

Psalm 105 is more joyful as it surveys Israel's wonderful history from the time of God's covenant with Abraham to the escape of the people from Egyptian slavery under the leadership of Moses.

> He led out his people rejoicing,
> his chosen ones in triumph.
> He gave them the lands of heathen nations;
> they took possession where others had toiled,
> so that they might keep his statutes
> and obey his laws.
> Praise the Lord.

We are wise always to pay due attention to the annals of the past, because they tell us much about human nature and therefore about ourselves also. How we respond to the records of the world's history is a good indication of our own inner attitudes, often concealed because of their disruptive power. Dreams can show us how we are functioning on a deeper, less rationally conscious level.

It is not inappropriate to deal finally with the present time, mirrored with thanksgiving in Psalm 66. The community thanks God for what he has done throughout the course of history as revealed in the present moment.

> Let all the earth acclaim God.
> Sing to the glory of his name,
> make his praise glorious.

The Psalmist remembers the two saving acts of God in the

history of Israel, the crossing of the Red Sea by Moses and
the people and then the passage over the Jordan by their
descendants with Joshua at the head of the hosts of Israel.

> Bless our God, you nations;
> let the sound of his praise be heard.
> He preserves us in life;
> he keeps our feet from stumbling.

God had proved a hard taskmaster, refining his people like
silver in various adversities, but now a place of plenty has
been reached. As a token of gratitude the usual animal sacrifices will be offered. But more important than this is the
nation's testimony to the world about the saving power of
God. Somewhat in the manner of Psalm 34, which enjoins
the right way of life, we read here:

> Come, listen, all who fear God,
> and I shall tell you what he has done for me;
> I lifted up my voice in prayer,
> his praise was on my tongue.
> If I had cherished evil thoughts,
> the Lord would not have listened;
> but in truth God did listen
> and paid heed to my plea.

In fact God never ceases to listen however subversive may be
our thoughts; were this not the case few of us would ever gain
the Lord's ear. But when our minds are turned away from
his excellence, there is less possibility of our hearing him.
Until we restore the relationship in humble penance our pleas
will bring no relief, for we will not hear the advice that is
being given us or receive the help that is always at hand. Our
lasting testimony of God's help is therefore an amended way
of life in which we follow the divine imperative to honesty
and love. Praising God is much to be recommended, but it
will remain hollow if it is not filled by such a love that will
not shrink from a total sacrifice of the individual for the sake

of his friends. These will be seen eventually to be all God's creatures and not only our human peers.

We may return with profit to where we started, the book of Ecclesiastes. The famous third chapter reminds us that everything has its season and every activity under heaven its time: a time to be born and a time to die. All the other categories subsequently listed are contingent on this first one. The psalms shed a perpetual light on the human situation, encouraging us in the day-to-day running of our lives. The Psalmist also suffered, but in the end a greater victory was his: immortality in this world as a writer of spiritual wisdom. We may trust that he knows immortality in the greater life beyond death also, something he could not grasp while in the flesh.

11

Of Places

To the Psalmist there is a place beyond peer, the Holy Land. Its paramount focus is Jerusalem with Mount Zion, and the ultimate centre is the Temple itself. How the Psalmist regards foreign soil by comparison with Israel is brought out starkly in Psalm 137, already mentioned on page 42 in connection with the feelings of vengeance that not infrequently colour the psalms, disfiguring it severely in this particular instance. The thought of singing a song of Zion to their captors in Babylon was intolerable to the exiles. The special relationship between God and Israel makes the very soil of that country blessed. Hence after Elisha's miraculous healing of Naaman the Aramaean army commander, the healed man takes soil from Israel (Samaria) to raise an altar to the one God in Damascus even though necessity obliges him also to show devotion to the local deity Rimmon, worshipped by the king of Aram (2 Kings 5:17–18). Concern for the things of the world is not to be disparaged provided prior acknowledgement is always afforded to the Creator.

One of the most beautiful of the Songs of the Ascents is Psalm 122:

> I rejoiced when they said to me,
> 'Let us go to the house of the Lord'.

In the pilgrimage they imagine they are already within Jerusalem's gates, the city is strong and restored. To it the tribes of Israel go up to give thanks to God, for there thrones of justice were set up. Then comes the most touching part of this short psalm:

Pray for the peace of Jerusalem:
'May those who love you prosper;
peace be within your ramparts
and prosperity in your palaces.'

Jerusalem is the City of Peace (Salem is sometimes used as
an abbreviation for the royal city, and it in turn is derived
from the Hebrew word 'Shalom', which means peace). One
can imagine the pilgrims halting at the gates of the city as
they hail it with shouts of 'Shalom'.

For the sake of these my brothers and my friends,
I shall say, 'Peace be within you.'
For the sake of the house of the Lord our God
I shall pray for your wellbeing.

The peace of Jerusalem invoked in this psalm brings us on
to the goodwill that should prevail among individual members
of the population. Psalm 133, the penultimate Song of the
Ascents, celebrates the brotherly love that should inform
the relationship between the priests and Levites serving in
the Temple, and by extension all true believers.

How good and how pleasant it is
to live together as brothers in unity!

Two analogies are made: the fragrant oil poured on the head
of Aaron and falling over his beard on to the collar of his
vestments, and the dew of Hermon falling on the mountains
of Zion. To me, the flow of oil or water, as the case may be,
signifies the downpouring of God's blessing on those who
work in a spirit of goodwill. To be sure, perfect peace is a
rare commodity, but it comes as a fruit of the Holy Spirit to
those who do the Lord's business unfailingly and without
fuss. The oil brings together Aaron and his brethren, signified
by the vestments he wears; the dew falls copiously on all the
ground of the mountains so that they become of one surface.

There the Lord bestows his blessing,
life for evermore.

Psalm 87 is a rousing eulogy of Zion:

The city the Lord founded stands on the holy hills.
He loves the gates of Zion
more than all the dwellings of Jacob.
Glorious things are spoken about you,
city of God.

There is a splendid universal scope as all the neighbouring nations are bidden to citizenship within Zion's boundaries. They are to declare allegiance to the one true God as the divine register includes them all in its pages.

Singers and dancers alike say,
'The source of all good is in you.'

The inclusion of all the surrounding peoples within the compass of Zion is indeed an attractive prospect. It is not God who excludes but man who will not enter. Entrance depends on something more than merely claiming the Lordship of the one God, mirrored in Jesus Christ in Christian theology. It involves growing into the stature of Christ by honourable behaviour and deep devotion to the truth as revealed both by the Church and one's inner light. The two, often with considerable discomfort, have to be reconciled and harmonized. The Church, which can be broadened to include organized religion in general, is often led astray by the temporal powers that surround it, so that it becomes party to terrible miscarriages of justice. The inner light can, on the other hand, become so inwardly directed that it loses contact with outer reality and degenerates into a focus of irrational prejudice. It should therefore be constantly challenged by the authority of an ongoing religious tradition whose validity has been proved by the witness of its saints and teachers. All this, in addition, has to be reconciled with the world view that at present prevails; nothing that lives can remain static for long.

The compilers of the Bible, for instance, knew very little about the world as compared with our own generation, and we may be sure that much more will be revealed provided we have the diligence and courtesy to attend to our labours day by day.

These reflections lead us on to another favourite psalm. Psalm 24 celebrates the glory of God as a prelude to the elect who may ascend the mountain of Zion and stand in the Temple:

> To the Lord belong the earth and everything in it,
> the world and all its inhabitants . . .
> Who may go up to the mountain of the Lord?
> Who may stand in his holy place?

The requirements remind us of Psalms 15 and 101: hands that are clean and a pure heart, a mind that is set on the truth only and whose word is reliable.

> Such a one shall receive blessing from the Lord, and be
> vindicated by God his saviour.

This is the good fortune of those who seek God in spirit and in truth, as we read later in John 4:24.

Then comes the fine antiphonal psalm as the servants of the Temple enter with solemnity:

> Lift up your heads, you gates,
> lift yourselves up, you everlasting doors,
> that the king of glory may come in.
> Who is this king of glory?
> The Lord strong and mighty,
> the Lord mighty in battle . . .
> Who is he, this king of glory?
> The Lord of Hosts, he is the king of glory.

It is possible that this latter part of the psalm dates from the translation of the Ark to Jerusalem commemorated in Psalm 132. The first part, whether or not of later date, reminds us

of the strict holiness required of those worshipping in the sight
of God. The prophets Amos, Hosea, Micah and Jeremiah all
are alike in arraigning ritual worship in the absence of a
penitent heart. It is all too easy to go through the motions of
religious devotion as a substitute for true worship in the truth
of one's condition and the spirit of holiness. Thus in the
already quoted Parable of the Publican and the Pharisee the
tax-gatherer's worship is faultless because he has given of his
very soul to God, whereas the pious Pharisee has given
nothing of himself though we may accept that his ritual
response has been excellent.

The mention of an elect who may ascend the mountain of
Zion and worship in the Temple strikes an unpleasant note
of élitism, but nevertheless we have to face the fact of the
great range of spiritual awareness in any group of people.
Jesus was not afraid to teach that the road that leads to life
is a narrow one and that those to be found on it are few in
comparison with the many travellers on the broad road that
leads to destruction (Matt. 7:13–14). However, those who do
elect to venture along the difficult path to spiritual proficiency
go of their own free will. They belong to no comfortable class
of society and gain little recognition for their efforts, at least
among their contemporaries. Among their number are natural
mystics to whom the presence of God is the only reality,
and also the enlightened sinners who have learnt by bitter
experience the folly of worldly gain and the necessity of love
before everything else. In other words, the elect are those who
have elected to follow the way of God, and they learn much
truth about themselves and the world around them as they
progress painfully up the narrow path to Mount Zion and
the eternal Temple at its peak.

Psalm 50 is itself a repetition of the teaching of the prophets
about the necessity of a clean heart before one worships God.

> God shines out from Zion, perfect in beauty.
> Our God is coming and will not keep silence . . .
> Listen, my people, and I shall speak;
> I shall bear witness against you, Israel:
> I am God, your God.

Then follows a scathing attack on the munificence of the animal sacrifices, the people being reminded that the Lord owns everything on earth already. What he wants is a sacrifice of thanksgiving and a fulfilment of the vows so earnestly made but so soon forgotten. Only then will God come to one's rescue, because only then will one be truly open to the divine love. By contrast the evildoer is roundly condemned for polluting the Temple worship with his gross hypocrisy. No amount of recitation of prayers will redeem the broken relationship with God; in one verse it is suggested that the wicked person actually thought God was someone like himself. Before we discard this suggestion as pure hyperbole, it is worthwhile remembering with shame the times when the larger Church has aligned itself with evil national powers and been an accessory to terrible destruction. The ambivalent attitude of most of the German Christian Church to Nazism is a case in point, but fortunately it has been counter-balanced by the heroic stand of various religious leaders in the opposition to injustice in many parts of the world. The witness is at present bearing impressive fruit. We all learn by experience, as the psalm is telling us:

> He honours me who offers a sacrifice of thanksgiving,
> and to him who follows my way
> I shall show the salvation of God.

It is not inappropriate that this psalm is followed by the great penitential Psalm 51.

Psalm 48 once again extols Zion, God's mountain:

> Great is the Lord and most worthy of praise
> in the city of our God.
> His holy mountain is fair and lofty,
> the joy of the whole earth.

The Psalmist sees Jerusalem as the city of the great King, while God as revealed in her palaces is a tower of strength. Then comes a commemoration of the stunning defeat of foreign rulers camped outside the city and waiting to conquer

it, an allusion, as in Psalm 46, to the Assyrian campaign
against the city and its literally miraculous deliverance by
God:

> See, the kings assemble;
> they advance together.
> They look, and are astounded;
> filled with alarm they panic.

Once this fearful threat has been removed there is sincere
devotion to God as the Psalmist meditates on the Lord's
steadfast love. One remembers how soon the divine inter-
vention is forgotten as apostasy follows thanksgiving, but
nevertheless, in the sheer relief of this feat of liberation, one
may rejoice in a mood of celebration, bringing with it one's
own act of homage for some recent trial successfully undergone.

> Go round Zion in procession,
> count the number of her towers,
> take note of her ramparts,
> pass her palaces in review,
> that you may tell generations yet to come
> that such is God,
> our God for ever;
> he will be our guide for evermore.

Psalm 74 reflects on Zion in a very different mood, one of
near despair after its desecration by the heathen. Why has
God deserted his flock that once he shepherded so lovingly;
why does he no longer remember the Temple which he
allowed to be made his temporal home in earlier times?

> Remember Mount Zion, which you made your
>   dwelling-place.
> Restore now what has been altogether ruined,
> all the destruction that the foe has brought on your
>   sanctuary.

At the present time the enemy fills the Temple with their shouts as they plant their standards as a token of victory. At the same time the fabric of the building is ruthlessly damaged as its most sacred precincts are wilfully destroyed. As in many psalms of lamentation, the enemy is identified as hostile to man no less than to God. Worse still, the age of great prophets is over, and who can tell how long this may last! One may add the ironical observation that a prophet never lacks honour except in his own time (in addition to his home town, his relations and his own family, as noted in Mark 6:4).

It is generally agreed that the occasion for this bitter psalm was the sack of the Temple by the mad hellenizing king Antiochus Epiphanes, mentioned on page 34 in connection with the Maccabaean revolt of the Jews, the role of martyrs, and the extended vision of the resurrection of the dead. During this terrible period of persecution the Temple gates were burnt and the sanctuary profaned. Later King Herod was to restore the Temple, which Jesus himself was to use as a place of teaching. The prophet had then indeed returned with a vengeance, but soon afterwards came the final destruction of the Temple in AD 70. A far more interior religion was to be practised by the Jews in their synagogues, the Christians in their churches, and at a later date by the Muslims in their mosques. They all arose from a common stock, and the agonies no less than the exultations of the Psalmist were to be part of the very fabric of their subsequent tradition.

It is worth noting the harsh words the Psalmist uses to God; there is no obsequious deference here. It gives us a clearer understanding of prayer when we observe this.

> Will the enemy pour scorn on your name for ever?
> Why do you hold back your hand,
> why keep your right hand within your bosom? . . .
> Rise up, God, defend your cause;
> remember how fools mock you all day long.
> Ignore no longer the uproar of your assailants,
> the ever-rising clamour of those who defy you.

We may end on a more hopeful note. The lovely Psalm

126, another of the Songs of the Ascents, recalls the return home of the Jewish exiles after the Babylonian captivity:

> When the Lord restored the fortunes of Zion,
> we were like people renewed in health.
> Our mouths were full of laughter,
> and our tongues sang aloud for joy.

Indeed the surrounding people were greatly impressed at what God had done for the Israelites. There follows a prayer that the people's fortunes may be restored, with the confident hope, always worth repeating:

> Those who sow in tears
> will reap with songs of joy.
> He who goes out weeping,
> carrying his bag of seed,
> will come back with songs of joy,
> carrying home his sheaves.

All this is excellent, but we must also look forward to the time when our enemies also may know the light of God's fortune, when the emotional separation that leads to enmity will have been transcended, when our adversaries will have taken their place in our lives as newly-found friends. This more universal gathering of an elect that includes everybody is not far from the vision of the finest psalms; it is explicitly articulated in Psalm 87, which we have considered earlier in this chapter.

History teaches us the evanescence of all worldly institutions. It is of interest how few of the worldly concerns of the Psalmist endured much after his time. Yet his love for the things around him is eternally valid. All earthly things are sacramental, being outer presages of the divine reality that far surpasses anything we can imagine on this side of the grave. St Paul, quoting Isaiah 64:4, writes of 'things beyond our seeing, things beyond our hearing, things beyond our imagining, all prepared by God for those who love him' (1 Cor. 2:9). But first we are to prove ourselves worthy by the care we bestow on the tangible products of our little world. In the thought of the Parable of the Talents (Matt. 25:14–30) the person who has shown himself worthy of the responsibility of looking after small things will be given a much greater work, as he comes and shares his master's joy. And so the ancient Jew's enthusiasm for the things of his country, and especially the Holy City with its dominating Temple, was not after all misplaced. The love he expended on the things that are past is now part of the spiritual atmosphere of mankind, inspiring generations who know little of that part of the world except by repute.

When a person of spiritual sensitivity visits a place of great devotion in past times, he can nearly always discern the holiness of the atmosphere, and this emanation accompanies him for the remainder of his life. As T. S. Eliot wrote in *Little Gidding*, 'You are here to kneel where prayer has been valid.' Ultimately such a place will not be special, such as the seventeenth-century religious community that Eliot remembered (and is happily reconstituted in the present time) or Mount Zion of old, but will be part of the general atmosphere in which we live and move and have our very existence, as St Paul spoke of God to the sceptical Athenians (Acts 17:28). While the Deity cannot be simply reduced to the form of a benign spiritual atmosphere, it is nevertheless in such an atmosphere that he shows himself most effectively to us. Then we may go about our business in the world intent on bringing our particular concern to fruition, so that the divine presence may be more accessible to those around us. In the work of intercessory prayer this presence may become universally active, until that time when the universe itself is freed from the shackles of mortality and is ready to enter upon the glorious liberty of the children of God (Rom. 8:21).

When the straggling remnant of the children of Israel returned home from exile, they felt disheartened when they remembered the glory of the Temple and beheld the rubble that now bore witness to its erstwhile existence. But God spoke through the prophet Haggai urging them to start on its reconstruction and assuring them of his support (Hag. 2:3–5). Then comes the promise (verses 6 to 9):

112

I shall shake the heavens and the earth, the sea and the dry land. I shall shake all the nations, and the treasure of all nations will come here; and I shall fill this house with splendour, says the Lord of Hosts. Mine is the silver and mine the gold, says the Lord of Hosts, and the splendour of this latter house will surpass the splendour of the former, says the Lord of Hosts. In this place I shall grant prosperity and peace.

Christ taught within its precincts, and now, though long destroyed in its physical form, it remains a psychical replica of the eternal place of God, which Moses was shown on Mount Sinai. Then he was instructed, 'See that you work to the design shown to you on the mountain' (Exod. 25:40).

In our own lives, times and places fade into oblivion with the passage of years and the increasing weakness of the body, but what we have learned and achieved during our period of activity we take with us, as we proceed along the narrow, uphill path of spiritual proficiency that brings us in conscious union with the One in whom alone we find eternal rest. And this rest is harmonious action in the service of all creation to the time of its own movement from death to immortality.

12

The Love of God

The love of God would appear to have two faces, our love of him and his love of us. We believe that God's love is eternal, unconditional and unrestricted, because his nature is love (1 John 4:16). We love because he loved us first (1 John 4:19). The explanation of this statement lies in our own inherent sinfulness which makes us unlovable by human standards. But the love of God can flow through us, evil as we may be, and then we realize that we are accepted by our Creator in our present state. Then there can be a progressive acceptance of our fundamental faults without flinching or self-justification. As we relax in the accepting love of God, so our defences begin to yield. Then at last we can start to relate to our fellows in calm acceptance of their natures, no longer either judging them adversely or feeling debased in front of them because we believe they are so much more spiritual than we are. This awareness is a presage of the peace that surpasses understanding which we are all to know at the end of time and the coming in glory of the Holy One.

God's love for his creation is expressed unforgettably in Psalm 103, which we have already considered on page 64 with regard to his support in times of trouble. Psalm 86 expresses some of the sentiments of the other psalm in the more taxing context of immediate trouble. The writer is poor and oppressed, and he calls for God's constant support:

> Fill your servant's heart with joy,
> for to you, Lord, I lift up my heart.
> Lord, you are kind and forgiving,
> full of love towards all who cry to you.

114

As in other psalms of entreaty, anxious descriptions of trouble are mixed with praise of God's power and requests for speedy relief:

Lord, listen to my prayer
and hear my pleading.
In the day of distress I call to you,
for you will answer me.
Among the gods not one is like you, Lord;
no deeds compare with yours.

As in Psalm 119, there is a request for God to teach the Psalmist his way that he may walk in his truth, and this is followed by thanks for the divine love and assistance. At once there is a lurid description of a band of evil men who are out to destroy the Psalmist and all he stands for in the great arena of life. As in Psalm 103, there is a description of God's nature, compassionate, gracious, long-suffering, ever faithful and true, and then follows the usual plea for protection. If only God would provide some sign of favour in the present emergency, so that the enemies may fall back abashed!

For you, Lord, have been my help and comfort.

The problem of God's silence when his beloved are in peril is perennial. It seems that we are being groomed for a more mature humanity, coping with our difficulties manfully without calling on the Lord for them simply to be removed. Prayer strengthens us immeasurably for the trials ahead, but it cannot be expected to solve our problems. If such a mechanism were in our grasp, we would casually take it for granted as our right, soon failing to exert ourselves to meet a difficult situation. As Jesus told his disciples, 'It is in your interest that I am leaving you. If I do not go, the advocate (the Holy Spirit) will not come, whereas if I go, I will send him to you' (John 16:7).

This is a hard lesson of love that all parents have eventually to learn: let the beloved alone to work out his own life's work. Bruised and battered, he may come closer to the God who absents himself for our sake than many would who were steeped in sincere piety but unable to make critical decisions on their own. Well does the writer of Ecclesiastes remark, 'He who keeps watching the wind will never sow, and he who keeps his eye on the clouds will never reap' (Eccles. 11:4). If we have faith in the overall efficient running of the universe, we can rely on our own acumen; things are bound to go wrong from time to time, but if we are wise, we can learn from the inevitable misfortunes of life so as to balance them with the times of plenty when we could give thanks with joy. Our trouble is a lack of awareness of the good fortune we so often experience; a decided reverse in events often makes us reflect on the golden past that had before been so taken for granted that its content lay forgotten in our minds.

It could be that the more moderate tone of the suffering writer of Psalm 86 reveals a grasp of this profound truth of life, so that he ceased to arraign God for his sufferings in the way that we have noted elsewhere, and started to see the divine relationship in a more sober light. I find this one of the most moving of the psalms of entreaty in the whole collection.

Many people find it hard, if not incomprehensible, to love God. They would truly yearn for the experience, but it seems to elude them. In this respect it is useful to understand what we call God in two modes. There is firstly the supreme unity which is beyond rational description; the great mystics have come closest to this ineffable splendour, and they agree that silence is the only mode in which the mystery can be disclosed. Yet, they cannot keep the experience to themselves, because a love of such intensity has overcome them that their dearest wish is to confide it to everyone around them. This is a fundamental property of love that it demands to be shared. The lover is in no way superior to the beloved, who is everyone, but his reward lies in imparting the healing grace of love to all who will receive it. 'Come for water, all who are thirsty; though you have no money, come, buy grain and eat; come, buy wine and milk, not for money, not for a price' (Isa. 55:1). The tragedy of love lies in the offhand, supercilious way it is treated:

He was in the world; but the world, though it owed its being to him, did not recognize him. He came to his own, and his own people would not accept him. But to all who did accept him, to those who put their trust in him, he gave the right to become children of God. (John 1:10–12)

The gift is, of course, free but the effect it has on the recipient transforms his whole life, so that he too is filled with love and participates in its flow to the whole world. It is in this spirit that our love for God becomes real.

And then the Deity ceases to be a mere ineffable atmosphere but becomes a living being. Love can never ignore the individual; it is essentially personal, unlike goodwill, which can remain diffuse and uncommitted despite all its fine aspirations. As articulate humans, we can hardly avoid describing the divine presence within us and around us in human terms; 'Father' is a favourite one, and will continue despite the family disarray that is such a prominent part of western society at present. The term father imparts strength, responsible guidance and protection, which is what we all need closest to our hearts. The term mother is also apposite; its tender, caring, nurturing character complements the directive strength of the masculine image, but does not supplant it. In fact both images are necessary (as the numerous mothers of one-parent families have to provide in our strangely amoral society). The parental archetype is deeply set in the personal as well as the collective unconscious, as is also the God-figure in the spirit of the soul. It is here that the divine essence is intimately known, but what is interior is merely a focus of the divine presence that transcends all finite being. The primordial unity may be called the Godhead, while its personal presence in the universe is the God who is worshipped in theistic religion, of which the psalms are outstanding examples. In Christian thought the God of religion is known in three personal forms: Father, Son and Holy Spirit, whereas in Judaism and Islam the one Father is known and glorified as God. Indeed the God of Islam is so transcendent that the metaphor Father may be considered impious by some

117

Muslims. Yet Allah too is described as the Merciful and Compassionate One, and is the focus of intense devotion.

The love of God beams on us when we are receptive to it. This means an inner silence, which we know in the first instance after wonder, gratitude or suffering have arrested our wandering thoughts in their tracks, and we are brought to stillness. Once we know the presence of love in that stillness, we respond in love to it, and our intimate response is called prayer. In prayer the mind and heart, indeed the whole being, is raised up to love of God. This in turn infuses the person, until eventually he gives the same love to God as he receives from him. St Bernard in a lovely sermon on the symbolism of the Canticles writes:

> The perfect correspondence of wills makes of two one spirit. We need not fear that the inequality of the two should make this harmony imperfect; love knows not reverence. Love is the great reality. It is the only affection of the soul in which the creature is able to respond to the Creator, though not on equal terms, and to repay like with like. Although being a creature the soul loves less, because she is less, nevertheless if she loves with her whole self, nothing is wanting where all is given. He that is joined to God is one spirit.

This quotation in *Mysticism in Religion* by W. R. Inge is followed by Inge's own reflection that although St Bernard speaks only of love to God, pure human love, as the sacrament of this, is the fulfilment of the law of love in our earthly life. He quotes Tertullian, 'When thou seest thy brother thou seest thy Lord.'

As we said at the beginning of the chapter, we love because he loved us first. The writer's love of God permeates all the psalms, but in a few, called the Psalms of Kingship, where God is celebrated as King of Israel, that devotion attains a peak. Our first chapter considered the glory of God as Creator of the universe with special reference to our little part of it. When we reflect on the theme of God as King, we find that his relationship with his creatures is seen in a more intimate way. They respond in love in the way that St Bernard described, and then the glory is infinite. Psalm 47 is the first, and magnificent it is too:

> Clap your hands, all you nations,
>   acclaim God with shouts of joy.
> How awesome is the Lord Most High,
>   great King over all the earth!

The universal scope of the psalm is noteworthy, as all people are summoned to applaud God. But he subdues all the other nations, choosing for Israel its heritage, the pride of Jacob whom he loves. There is a shout of triumph as God rises and goes up to the Temple in a great procession, and cries of great praise accompany the procession. God is King of the whole earth, and the people are urged to sing psalms for all they are worth.

> Seated on his holy throne,
> God reigns over the nations.

The rulers of all the nations assemble with the Israelites to do him homage, for the mighty ones of earth belong to God, who is exalted on high. This is no ritual act, such as the prophets often deprecated. The joy surges through the assembled mass as they make their acclamation about the God whom they love and cherish as one with themselves.

Psalm 93 in tones of magisterial authority declares God's Kingship:

> The Lord has become King, clothed with majesty;
>   the Lord is robed, girded with might.

In rather the same way as Psalm 29 (see page 10) God is seen as the master of the power that controls the world. The crashing breakers of the sea are as nothing compared with the might and majesty of the Creator, while the earth is immovably established. Like Psalm 19, with which we began our reflections on the psalms, the Law is juxtaposed with the natural order, whose laws too are under divine control:

> Your decrees stand firm,
> and holiness befits your house,
> Lord, throughout the ages.

From all eternity God is Lord, his throne being established from of old.

Psalm 96 once again celebrates God's universal majesty:

> Sing a new song to the Lord.
> Sing to the Lord, all the earth.
> Sing to the Lord and bless his name;
> day by day proclaim his victory . . .
> Ascribe to the Lord, you families of nations,
> ascribe to the Lord glory and might . . .
> Bring an offering and enter his courts;
> in holy attire worship the Lord;
> tremble before him, all the earth.
> Declare among the nations, 'The Lord is King.'

Once again the imagery of Psalm 29 is used to describe the omnipotence of the Lord. And then follows a sequence of judgement:

> 'He will judge the peoples with equity.'
> Let the heavens rejoice and the earth be glad,
> let the sea resound and everything in it . . .
> before the Lord when he comes,
> when he comes to judge the earth.
> He will judge the world with justice
> and peoples by his faithfulness.

The judgement of God is the Law, but once we have moved into the realm of love, the Law is fulfilled inasmuch as a person of love cannot contravene the moral imperatives of God's Law as revealed to Moses. St Paul amplifies this theme in Romans 13:8–10. When these psalms of God's Kingship were recited, the Jews were filled with the love of God. It is not surprising that the usual national exclusiveness broke down into a worldwide outlook that could embrace all peoples in God's Kingdom. It reminds us today also that love alone can heal the terrible rifts among the various nations of the world. Religions are valid in so far as they stimulate this love by the disciplines of prayer, communal worship and service in the greater community. Love in fact transcends credal barriers by fulfilling the creed and expanding it to embrace all humanity.

Psalm 97 continues the theme of divine Kingship. It is in fact an amalgam of other psalm texts:

> The Lord has become King; let the earth be glad,
> let coasts and islands all rejoice.
> Cloud and thick mist enfold him,
> righteousness and justice
> are the foundation of his throne . . .
> The heavens proclaim his righteousness,
> and all peoples see his glory.

All idols and false gods are castigated; they collapse into non-existence in the presence, the face, of the living God. Great was the greeting of Judah's cities at the name of God, for he is a refining fire and also a refreshing breeze. The evildoers are hated, but God's loyal servants are kept safe, a debatable doctrine considered in greater detail on pages 32 and 57.

> A harvest of light has arisen for the righteous,
> and joy for the upright in heart.
> You that are righteous, rejoice in the Lord
> and praise his holy name.

Psalm 95 is the most familiar of the set, since it is often used in the course of morning prayer in Christian worship. It is called the *Venite*.

> Come! Let us raise a joyful song to the Lord,
> a shout of triumph to the rock of our salvation.

Let us come into his presence with thanksgiving
and sing psalms of triumph to him.
For the Lord is a great God,
a great King above all gods.

He is the Creator of all the world, and we are bidden to enter
into the Temple and bow down in worship before the God
who made us, who shepherds his flock with tender care. It is
this part of the psalm that is recited during morning worship;
the remainder is optional because it describes the wrath of
God with destructive vigour. It recalls the backsliding of the
people during the exodus from Egypt, how God abhorred
them for their ingratitude, and saw to it that none of them
should enter the divine rest.

It is quite right that a temporal king should show his anger,
because he is, after all, only human like the rest of us. But
wrath of the intensity described in Psalm 95 ill befits the God
of love celebrated in Psalm 103 and the passages from St
John's first letter quoted at the beginning of this chapter. The
wrath of God has been equated with his 'jealousy', revealed
to Moses on Mount Sinai, but this again needs careful
interpretation. A devoted parent is jealous of his child's reputation, and will punish him severely for a misdemeanour. We
have considered this on pages 98–9 but the rage depicted in
some of the psalms, as in the other parts of the Bible, has not
been ultimately helpful to the propagation of higher religion.
It is, I believe, best to see the law of the universe as the
agent of punishment, as the civil law and its servants necessarily punish us if we contravene it. But God transcends his
creation; while being intimately concerned in its welfare, he
does not interfere in its working. He can, however, be called on
in prayer, and then pours his Spirit on to us as we work more
harmoniously for the common good. Love accepts us for what
we are in order to direct us to what we are to become, true
children of God in the image of his incarnate Son Jesus.
Every action has its effect, but no effect is outside the divine
compassion and assistance provided we ask in humble faith.
One must hope that the many recalcitrant Israelites who
apostasized so often in the wilderness on the way to the Holy

Land were able to repent of their folly in the greater life beyond death. Such, at any rate, is the hope expressed in 2 Maccabees 12:38–45. The wisdom of inner knowledge that comes with the ageing process tells us that either heaven is for us all or else none can be worthy of it. A heaven in which even one creature was excluded would be intolerable to those inside its bounds, since love is the very essence of the heavenly state.

Psalm 100 is also familiar through morning worship. It is called the *Jubilate:*

> Let all the earth acclaim the Lord!
> Worship the Lord in gladness;
> enter his presence with joyful songs.

We are exhorted to acknowledge the Kingship of God, that he made us. In its origin the psalm implies that the Israelites were his own people, the flock which he shepherds, but we now can extend this to the whole human race, and through its ministry to the entire created order. It was the privilege of Israel to bring this knowledge of God to the remainder of the world, finally through the ministry of Jesus and Muhammad.

> Enter his gates with thanksgiving,
> his courts with praise.
> Give thanks to him and bless his name;
> for the Lord is good and his love is everlasting,
> his faithfulness endures to all generations.

The first part of the last sentence is repeated throughout the Old Testament: Jeremiah 33:11 and Ezra 3:11 are good examples. The pairing of love and faithfulness, noted in Psalm 89, reaches its fulfilment here.

Psalms 98 and 99 are also psalms of God's Kingship. The first stresses God's judgemental activities in the world, while the second exalts his holiness. In his might the King loves justice and has established equity. We should bow in homage at his footstool. Then comes the memory of the work of Moses and Aaron, who were his priests, and also Samuel, a devoted minister of the Lord. They called and he answered in the pillar of cloud, which is, in fact, the divine darkness of the mystic, the cloud of unknowing written about by the unknown English medieval spiritual genius.

Psalm 99 notes that although God answered his servants, he also called them to account for their misdeeds, but he then forgave them. No matter how ardent we are in the spiritual life, we may be sure that the coarser 'outer man' will make his protests from time to time. If we take ourselves too seriously, we may begin to despair of ever making progress on the inner path. And then the Lord, who is the master of good humour among other things, will smile lovingly at us, and tell us to proceed onwards. Of course we are unworthy of our universal priestly calling, but he is worthy. All he wants of us is our attention, so that we may do the present work as efficiently as possible. If it is done in his name, we may be sure that it will be well done, and a blessing will flow out to us in its performance. 'Put me to the proof, says the Lord of Hosts, and see if I do not open windows in the sky and pour a blessing on you as long as there is need' (Mal. 3:10). But first we must bring the whole tithe into the treasury, so that there may be food for God's house, which is the eternal Temple.

13

To the Praise of God

There is a difference between thanksgiving and praise: thanksgiving, or gratitude, is an expression of unbounded joy for a gift of God, whereas praise is a greater expression of joy for God's supreme gift of himself to us. We considered the way in which God reveals himself to us in the previous chapter: a presence beyond description which fills us with such love that we cannot contain its strength within ourselves, but are constrained to share it with all those around us. God is in essence unknowable except by the energies that proceed from the presence of the Godhead. The two great energies are love and light, the second of which is common to all genuine mystical experience, and shows itself in the world of form as enlightenment, as wisdom, as understanding, and, as we touch solid earth, knowledge of material things. Yet paradoxically, the greatest knowledge is unitive knowledge between two people and between man and God. This knowledge is true love, a love so intense that it brings the whole creation into harmony, so that everything works with a common purpose of fulfilment. The end is the transfiguration of the world into spiritual radiance, the same radiance that Peter, James and John were privileged to see when their Master revealed his divinity to them on Mount Tabor (Matt. 17:1–8; Mark 9:2–8; Luke 9:28–36). The end of celebrating the divine Kingship is sheer praise that God is God and thanksgiving that he has given himself unreservedly to us in the supreme gift of life, of human freedom, and above all in the form of his Son. The Psalmist, of course, could not grasp this last gift, whereby we may all come to share in the very being of God

(2 Peter 1:4), but he can glimpse it in the depth of holiness of the greatest of his writings.

A muted psalm of praise is Psalm 63. It is a desperate yearning for God in the wilderness of life and praise that he is as he is, and a constant bastion for us in our trials:

> God, you are my God; I seek you eagerly
> with a heart that thirsts for you
> and a body wasted with longing for you,
> like a dry land, parched and devoid of water.

God's love is unfailing and better than life itself, therefore the writer sings his praises:

> Thus all my life I bless you;
> in your name I lift my hands in prayer.
> I am satisfied as with a rich feast
> and there is a shout of praise on my lips.

We remember the cry of Psalm 23, when the writer rejoices in God's spreading a table for him in his enemies' presence, but here there is no feeling of revenge, only a remembered delight in God's presence. Indeed, in that holy presence, all earthly encounters, unpleasant as they may be, are lifted up into a celestial harmony, such as we may know in worldly life when we awake from an untroubled sleep. I have long regarded sleep as one of God's most beautiful gifts to us, and if, like Shelley, we may see death as its brother, we can follow the tortuous course of mortal life with greater equanimity. But such a sleep is well earned inasmuch as we have come to terms with ourselves and the life we have led. We give this to God as our humble sacrifice, and in turn he gives us himself, as he did the repentant publican whom we have considered on numerous occasions throughout this book.

> I call you to mind on my bed
> and meditate on you in the night watches,
> for you have been my help
> and I am safe in the shadow of your wings.

There, alas, follows a stanza of imprecation against the Psalmist's enemies, but the end is the triumph of the king and those who swear justly by God's name. The psalm shows us, once again, how labile are human emotions: glorious praise can so soon be followed by cursing of our fellows. It takes a long time to attain the Christian ideal, 'Love your enemies and pray for your persecutors' (Matt. 5:44). God does indeed cause the sun to rise on good and bad alike, and sends rain on both innocent and wicked. It is what we do with God's bounty that determines the course of our life and the prospect ahead of us when earthly things have faded away and pure spirit awaits us. Our hope lies in the conversion of all that is corrupt rather than its destruction, because violence gives rise to more violence, and hatred foments so much antagonism that total destruction can easily follow. In our own century these statements are no longer merely otherworldly theories but stark truths. This should cause us no surprise, because God loves everything he has created, and love does not countenance destruction. It works for healing, transformation and ultimate resurrection.

The great psalms of praise are the 'Hallels' that the community of Israel recited at the great feasts or in the morning. They are Psalms 113 to 118, 136, and 146 to 150. The 'Lesser Hallel' are Psalms 113 to 118, and they are followed by Psalm 136, the 'Great Hallel', especially at the Passover meal. Jesus and the disciples recited them at the fateful meal when the Eucharist was instituted (Matt. 26:30). Psalm 113 praises God with the customary imagery of cosmic glory, but then it stoops to the lowly person also:

> There is none like the Lord our God
> in heaven or on earth,
> who sets his throne so high
> but deigns to look down so low;
> who lifts the weak out of the dust
> and raises the poor from the rubbish heap,
> giving them a place among princes,
> among the princes of his people;

who makes the woman in a childless house
a happy mother of children.

The poor and weak may have been the returned exiles from
Babylon who attained power in the newly restored Holy Land
(under Persian rule), but they are even more those among us
who have suffered pain or humiliation (as did Sarah and
Hannah because of their sterility) and then through God's
grace and their own courage (a virtue never lacking in the
Jews throughout their long history of travail) have come to a
greater knowledge of reality. These are the real princes of the
people, for they can dispense God's gifts in a way that goes
beyond personal striving.

Psalm 114 has a typical Passover theme, for it celebrates
the exodus from Egypt. Especially delightful is the use of
vivid similies:

> The mountains skipped like rams,
> the hills like lambs of the flock.
> What made you, the sea, flee away?
> Jordan, what made you turn back?
> Why did you skip like rams, you mountains,
> and like lambs, you hills?

Psalm 115 once again glorifies God:

> Why should the nations ask,
> 'Where, then, is their God?'
> Our God is high in heaven;
> he does whatever he wills.

His power is compared with the impotence of the idols worshipped by other nations. By contrast, the Jews and those
friendly with them (the proselytes) trust in the one true (and
only) God, who is their help and shield. In God there is the
blessing of life, fertility, and joy. The end of the psalm contrasts the dead who can no longer praise the Lord, with the
living who can exult in his presence now and for ever more.
To the ancient Jew death may well have meant a cessation

of relationship with God and man, but we can see this death more in terms of the voluntary break in relationship with God that follows a sinful action. While we persist in our wickedness, we imprison ourself in the silent grave, but once we confess our sins we move into life once more, a life that knows no ending in its promise and glory.

Psalm 116 is one of thanksgiving to God for a rescue from death's cords. The expressions of relief are very real:

> Gracious is the Lord and righteous;
> our God is full of compassion.
> The Lord preserves the simple-hearted;
> when I was brought low, he saved me.

God's deliverance has brought peace to the writer's heart, for now he can walk in the divine presence in the land of the living. He will thank God by the offering of libations; these are drink offerings:

> I shall lift up the cup of salvation
> and call on the Lord by name.
> I shall pay my vows to the Lord
> in the presence of all his people.
> A precious thing in the Lord's sight
> is the death of those who are loyal to him.

This was because death severed the connection between creature and Creator, at least in the primitive Israelite understanding, so rooted were the people to the awareness of the physical body. Now we can see this lovely sentence as a homage to the martyrs of every age, witnesses to the truth and not ashamed to die for it. But we now know, with a knowledge that comes of deep love, that they are exalted members of the Communion of Saints and that their intercessions are as important for us as ours are for those in pain among us in this earthly domain. In his release from suffering the Psalmist himself has passed from death to an expanded life in which he can pay his vows conscientiously 'in the presence of all God's people, in the courts of the Lord's house, in the midst of you, Jerusalem. Alleluia.' This last word means 'Praise the Lord'.

Psalm 117 is the shortest of all the psalms. It exhorts all nations to praise the Lord and to extol him, for his protecting love is as strong as his faithfulness is everlasting. The universal outlook of this tiny psalm is noteworthy.

Psalm 118 is a fitting zenith to the climax of praise; it is a processional hymn for the feast of Tabernacles:

> It is good to give thanks to the Lord,
> for his love endures for ever.
> Let Israel say:
> 'His love endures for ever.'
> Let the house of Aaron say:
> 'His love endures for ever.'
> Let those who fear the Lord say:
> 'His love endures for ever.'

There then follows an account of God's help when the writer was in distress:

> With the Lord on my side, I am not afraid;
> what can mortals do to me? . . .
> It is better to seek refuge in the Lord
> than to trust in any mortal,
> better to seek refuge in the Lord
> than to trust in princes.

The Israelites, personified in the Psalmist, overcame the relentless assaults of the enemy, because God came to their help and proved their refuge and deliverer. The Lord may indeed have chastened the nation, but he would not see its destruction. In terms reminiscent of Psalm 24 he says:

> Open to me the gates of victory;
> I shall go in by them and praise the Lord.

Then comes a famous theme with strong Messianic overtones:

> The stone which the builders rejected
> has become the main corner-stone.
> This is the Lord's doing;
> it is wonderful in our eyes.

In the immediate context the main corner-stone can be likened to Israel, apparently rejected in Babylon but now reinstated as the keystone in God's Temple. But it is also a stone of stumbling for those who are unaware of God's grace. In Isaiah 8:14 we read that God will become a snare, an obstacle, and a rock against which the two houses of Israel will strike and stumble, if he is not obeyed and revered in performing the correct action. It is God, not any people, who is the keystone, and if he is disobeyed, events will crash down upon the heedless throng. God shows himself in his chosen people and finally in the form of his beloved Son Jesus of Nazareth. In this world nothing may be taken for granted; on the contrary, even the meanest particle should be lifted up and cherished for the time of its own resurrection into the light of God. The Psalmist continues:

> Blessed is he who enters in the name of the Lord;
> we bless you from the house of the Lord.
> The Lord is God; he has given us light.
> Link the pilgrims with cords
> as far as the horns of the altar.

The cords are branches of myrtle or palm waved by the pilgrims as the procession circled the altar, the ritual of the *lulah*, the joyful march of the people in the Temple commemorating the period in the wilderness when their ancestors lived in tents made of leaves. At that time they had no permanent dwellings such as they were later to inhabit when they came to the Promised Land. And yet, they were more securely ensconced in the wilderness than in Caanan, for the Lord was more immediately with them during the exodus than later, when they were seduced by the local deities and fell repeatedly into apostasy. The liturgy of the feast of Tabernacles is defined in Leviticus 23:39–43.

131

Before the part of the psalm quoted above comes the supplication:

> Lord, deliver us, we pray;
> Lord, grant us prosperity.

The first sentence is the *Hosanna*, to which the priests respond with a blessing. It was shouted by the crowds on what was destined to be called Palm Sunday, when Jesus rode into Jerusalem mounted on a donkey. By that time the *Hosanna* was more an acclamation than a prayer (Matt. 21:9).

Psalm 136, the Great Hallel, is recited after the series of psalms that constitute the Lesser Hallel at the Passover meal. It is in the form of a litany, a series of petitions or (in this instance) exultations recited by the clergy and responded to, usually in repeated formulas, by the congregation.

> It is good to give thanks to the Lord,
> for his love endures for ever.
> Give thanks to the God of gods;
> his love endures for ever.
> Give thanks to the Lord of lords –
> his love endures for ever;
> who alone works great marvels –
> his love endures for ever.

And so the psalm proceeds, first celebrating the prodigies of creation itself – as described at the beginning of the Book of Genesis – and then recalling the events of the great exodus from Egypt. There are no half measures in the Psalmist's praise; he enjoys the discomfiture and destruction of Israel's foes with a savage relish. But it is good that the psalm ends on a more universal note:

> He gives food to all mankind;
> his love endures for ever.
> Give thanks to the God of heaven,
> for his love endures for ever.

Personally I find this type of victory ode quite acceptable in its own context inasmuch as our first concern is to keep alive. If we are threatened with our very survival by murderous hordes, it is necessary that they should be put in their place. It is not unreasonable to remember our victory and praise God for it. This is the lesson of history, and the Old Testament is one immense study of the history of a single remarkable nation. But after the victory ode there must be an elegy for the vanquished also; only occasionally does the biblical record rise to this height. Isaiah 19:19–24 is a noteworthy exception; its conclusion is quite remarkable. 'When that day comes Israel will rank as a third with Egypt and Assyria and be a blessing in the world. This is the blessing the Lord of Hosts will give: "Blessed be Egypt my people, Assyria my handiwork, and Israel my possession." ' The fulfilment of this prophecy of more than 2,500 years ago is still eagerly awaited. Only when the God of love is allowed to enter the hearts of all his people can this state of peace and acceptance be brought about. Then even the cruelty of persecution will have been forgiven in the light of the greater forbearance that it taught its victims. But we must frankly admit that bearing grievances and nursing old scores is much more immediately satisfying than learning to accept injustice and proceed on our journey with gratitude that we are alive. Forgiveness comes from God, and it tends to dawn on us as a blessed release when our tension is at its tightest. The old victories that Jesus and his disciples were remembering on the night of the Last Supper were soon to be illuminated by his own supreme victory over the concerted psychic evil of the cosmos as he strove alone at Gethsemane.

We may profitably leave this reflection on praise to God by considering Psalm 138. Unlike the Hallels, this is a very personal communication with God:

> I shall give praise to you, Lord, with my whole heart;
> in the presence of the gods I shall sing psalms to you.
> I shall bow down towards your holy temple;
> for your love and faithfulness I shall praise your name.

The Psalmist's exultation follows God's help in a difficult situation so that he was strengthened for the trial. The kings are exhorted to extol God, who also cares for the lowly while taking note of the ways of the arrogant. As in Psalm 63, the praise of God has a note of fear and beseeching, this time right at the end:

> The Lord will accomplish his purpose for me.
> Your love endures for ever, Lord;
> do not abandon what you have made.

It is always a good thing to be able to praise a person. We are paying homage to him and, by implication, to what he stands for. We gain nothing from him on an acquisitive level, but his presence, or the witness of his works, fills us with joy. This is translated practically in a fresh resolve to actualize our own talents to their maximum, so that we may, however humbly, participate in the joy we have been given.

So also do we flow out in praise to God for being what he is. We start by praising him for his marvellous works; we end by praising him for himself alone. This is the apogee of love, for in this action we have pledged ourselves to do our best to walk in the divine presence and do what he would want us to do. What God wants of us is first that we should be fulfilled in our own being, and second that we should bring that fulfilment into whatever situation we may find ourselves. The psalms are excellent examples of what this may mean in everyday life. Though the Psalmist may complain, grumble and curse all adverse circumstances in his life, he still keeps faith with God, who so often seems to hide himself from human suffering, as he appeared to do when Jesus hung miserably from his cross (Mark 15:33–37). But only when God is apparently unavailable can we get on with our own work. In fact, of course, he has never left us, but now we have to learn to find him in the depths of our own being. When we have made this great discovery, we can certainly shout for joy, for we know we are always cared for, and as St Paul puts its so memorably:

TO THE PRAISE OF GOD

I am convinced that there is nothing in death or life, in the realm of spirits or superhuman powers, in the world as it is or the world as it shall be, in the forces of the universe, in heights or depths – nothing in all creation that can separate us from the love of God in Christ Jesus our Lord. (Rom. 8:38–39)

14

The Joy of Life

Psalms 146 to 150 constitute, as we mentioned in chapter 13, a third Hallel, recited by the Jews in the morning. Their message is not very different from that of Psalms 113 to 118 and Psalm 136, yet somehow their impact is more immediate, more pertinent for our present situation. While God's help to his people Israel in the past is not overlooked, it is his eternal presence in the fleeting life of the world that is especially celebrated. One can almost see the person, freshly awake from a good night's sleep, exulting in the promise of a new day's experience.

Psalm 146 praises God for all he does at any time:

> As long as I live I shall praise the Lord;
> I shall sing psalms to my God all my life long.
> Put no trust in princes
> or in any mortal, for they have no power to save.

Indeed they are mere mortals, and their plans, exalted though they may be, do not survive their own transience. It may well be that someone else takes over the project, but its subsequent shape will be very different from that envisaged by its initiator. When we consider the amazing history of the Church in respect of the life and teaching of its Founder, we may well wonder at the spiritual impotence of human endeavour, so often corrupted by avarice and the lust for power. But even in its moral extremity God has been with her, for his Spirit sustains her integrity, sometimes in the face of an intransigent hierarchy.

The writer goes on to extol the unique power of God, our

only true hope and helper, who not only is the supreme
Creator but also stoops to deal out justice to the oppressed,
feed the hungry, restore sight to the blind, and raise the bent
and humiliated. He supports all those who are weak: the
stranger, the fatherless and the widow, while thwarting the
course of the wicked. How, it may well be asked, does the
Lord perform these various works of goodness? It is through
the agency of humans that charity flows. It is especially the
prerogative of the Messiah to undertake these great works:
Isaiah 11:1–9 and 61:1–3 (quoted in Luke 4:18–19 in respect
of Christ's mission) are key texts. But through the divine
indwelling of the Holy Spirit we too are expected to carry on
the work of God. The ethical psalms, such as 15, 24 and 101,
stress the negative side of this commitment: that we should
neither do nor countenance any base action. The Parable of
the Sheep and the Goats (Matt. 25:31–46) points to the positive requirements already defined in Psalm 146. We must
feed the hungry, give drink to those who thirst, house the
stranger, clothe the naked, help the sick and visit the prisoner.
The reason is that God in Christ is immanent in all human
souls, even if the perverted will refuses to acknowledge him
and proceeds in its own destructive way. But a time of reckoning will come, as it did to the Prodigal Son, and then a firm
decision will have to be made. We may hope that all of us
will return to the Father, as he did in the famous parable
(Luke 15:11–32). The divine forgiveness does not harden, but
the human arrogance may persist indefinitely. Pride is indeed
the foremost of the seven deadly sins.

Psalm 147 is particularly delightful, juxtaposing God's
mighty creative acts, which never come to an end since the
present disposition of the elements is part of the ongoing
creation of the universe, with his fatherly care for his people:

> It is he who heals the broken in spirit
> and binds up their wounds,
> who numbers the stars one by one
> and calls each by name . . .
> The Lord gives support to the humble
> and brings evildoers to the ground.

The description of God's creation is especially fine, reminding us of Psalm 104 in its vivid evocation of the natural scene:

> He veils the sky in clouds
> and provides rain for the earth;
> he clothes the hills with grass.
> He gives food to the cattle
> and to the ravens when they cry.

Yet God is not impressed with the horse's strength or the runner's speed; what he desires is the fear (which is best understood as respect) of his rational creatures who wait for his steadfast love. This respect shows itself in a sense of awesome responsibility as we in turn play our part in assisting God's unceasing activity. We do this both by conserving the present structure and by being open to new directives of the Holy Spirit. It is thus that human creativity finds its natural fulfilment.

> He sends his command over the earth,
> and his word runs swiftly.
> He showers down snow, white as wool,
> and sprinkles hoar-frost like ashes;
> he scatters crystals of ice like crumbs;
> he sends the cold, and the water stands frozen.

This fine description of the cold reminds us of a somewhat similar revelation of God's creative power to Job near the beginning of the great theophany (the appearance of God to man) that forms the peak of that great Wisdom book (Job 37:10 and 38:22).

The psalm concludes with a touching reminder of Israel's election:

> To Jacob he reveals his word,
> his statutes and decrees to Israel;
> he has not done this for other nations,
> nor were his decrees made known to them.

St Paul would reply that in Christ a universal knowledge of God's love and wisdom has become available to gentile as well as Jew, but in fact much spiritual spadework still needs to be done before the depth of this knowledge will become accessible to all people. It seems as if a Job type of experience is still necessary to open human eyes to the spiritual foundation of the world.

Psalm 148 is a cosmic hymn of praise:

> Praise the Lord from the heavens;
> praise him in the heights above.
> Praise him, all his angels;
> praise him, all his hosts.

All the supramundane creation is summoned to praise God, for he is their eternal Creator. And so all the earth's creatures are called to praise God also, sea monsters and ocean depths, fire and hail, snow and ice and gales of wind. Then follow the earthly inhabitants, animals of various kinds, kings and commoners, princes and rulers, boys and girls, old and young. All are summoned to praise the name of the Lord, whose name is high above all others, and whose majesty extends beyond the created universe. As in Psalm 147, there is a final allusion to Israel's special position with God;

> He has exalted his people in the pride of power
> and crowned with praise his loyal servants,
> Israel, a people close to him.

Psalm 149 has a national theme. The Israelites' privilege is celebrated: they are to be the instrument of God's justice against the pagan nations, looking towards the latter days of mankind. This eschatology, the doctrine of the last things, is prominent in the prophetic writings, especially those of Ezekiel, and is the great theme of the latter part of the Book of Daniel. This finds its New Testament counterpart in the Revelation of John which concludes the Bible. The people of Israel are called on to rejoice in God their maker, to praise his name (which means his nature, for the Lord can have no tangible name that may be misused by thoughtless humans) in dancing and song. God accepts his people, and crowns the lowly with victory. The psalm ends on a belligerent note: the people carry a two-edged sword to wreak vengeance on the nations, so carrying out the judgement decreed against them. This is the glory for all God's loyal servants.

In a strange way this does seem to have been the destiny of the Jews, although their witness to the truth has been one of suffering and martyrdom rather than the military power envisaged in the psalm. Though they have been driven from pillar to post, expelled from one country after another in their chequered history since the destruction of the Temple in AD 70, they have survived as a small but spiritually vital witness, while their various persecutors lie dead in the dust of history.

Psalm 150 is a final chorus of praise, the zenith of the gradually mounting climax building up in its four predecessors. God is to be praised in his holy place and in the vault of heaven, he is to be praised for his acts of power and his immeasurable greatness. Every musical instrument is to take part in this mighty chorus of praise: fanfares on the trumpet, on harp and lyre, with tambourines and dancing, with flute and strings, and with clashing cymbals.

Let everything that has breath praise the Lord!

So ends this elaborate doxology, the liturgical formula of praise to God.

The joy of sheer living is, of course, expressed in many less emotionally charged psalms. Psalm 23 delights in God's abundant providence as we live soberly and do our work diligently: the Lord is our shepherd, and in him we lack for nothing. The images of green pastures in which to lie down, and water in which to rest impart trust and warmth as we proceed onwards in a world that is by no means encouraging to spiritual aspiration. Even the thought of travelling through a dark valley causes little disturbance when we know that God, with his shepherd's staff and crook, is near us. Though we may be of small consequence in the world's eyes, we are important to our Creator, who protects each of us at all times, possibly by the mediation of a special guardian angel.

Psalm 49 shows us where true joy is to be found:

> Why should I be afraid in evil times
> when beset by the wickedness of treacherous foes,
> trusting in their wealth
> and boasting of their great riches?

The writer reminds us that no one could ever ransom himself nor pay God the price of his release, for the ransom would be too high. We all share a common destiny, death and oblivion, at least from the memories of all those apart from our loved ones. All we once had falls into other people's hands, a theme we have considered in a slightly different context on page 111. The Psalmist uses an ironical dictum both in the middle of the psalm and at its end:

> For human beings like oxen are short-lived;
> they are like beasts whose lives are cut short.

Such is the fate of the fool who depends on material support. He will die like those before him, and be swallowed up in the sea of oblivion.

> But God will ransom my life
> and take me from the power of Sheol.

And so we are not to envy the selfish, affluent person whose end is lamentable no matter how well he may live at present. In God alone is joy, and in his service is that real freedom to give of ourself unashamedly for the benefit of our fellow creatures. In the end this is the only joy, for its end product is a transformed world. As Jesus put it in the story of Zacchaeus, the very rich superintendent of taxes who was converted to honest living, 'Today salvation has come to this house – for this man too is a son of Abraham. The Son of Man has come to seek and to save what is lost' (Luke 19:9–10). The joy of the father of the Prodigal Son, pacifying the virtuous older brother, when the scapegrace returns, has a similar ring: 'How could we fail to celebrate this happy day? Your brother here was dead and has come back to life; he was lost and has been found' (Luke 15:32).

15

Epilogue

The psalms take us through the full gamut of human experience and show us the ambivalent quality of our dedication to the highest. We too are the victims of our emotions and their prisoner also. Only occasionally we are privileged to escape the vicious circle of cause and effect. This occurs when our minds and hearts are lifted up to God. Then at last can we discern what is real and imperishable in a world where outer appearance is the god that governs the lives and actions of its creatures. The movement from the temporal to the eternal is accomplished in contemplative prayer, but until this contemplative awareness is part of our daily life, we will slip back insidiously into the prison of outer appearance.

The Old Testament, except for Daniel 12:2; 2 Maccabees 7:9–36 and 14:46; and Wisdom 3:1–9 (all of which are late writings, dating from less than 200 years before the Christian era), has little to say about the life beyond death, even though the Psalmist, as we have seen, does occasionally yearn for an indissoluble union with his Creator. This somewhat materialistic outlook is, in fact, less unspiritual than appears at first sight. The more we grasp for proof of survival of death, the more tantalizingly ambivalent does the evidence show itself. The person who is most convinced about personal survival is the one who is so fully about his Father's business that he has no time for selfish aspirations. As Dante wrote in the *Paradiso* section of *The Divine Comedy*, 'In His will is our peace.' When love fills our souls, we have already passed from death to eternal life, to paraphrase 1 John 3:14.

There is indeed only one life, which is eternal. Worldly existence, death of the physical body, and life in the greater world beyond that death are all part of the pageant of eternal life as pertains to our small but important experience on the solid earth. Those who are in touch with their own identity know inwardly that they are immortal; it is what we do with that immortality that matters, for it can as easily be a prison as a delight. In God our immortality thrusts through the time barrier and enters eternal life now, rather like a vigorous bud bursting through the protecting whorl of sepals to reveal its petals, the beauty of the open flower.

When we read the psalms we may think of the bud just about to burst into bloom. This event was the incarnation of Christ, who came to fulfil the Law that could as easily be a prison as a way to joyful living, if it were obeyed to the letter while its spirit was denied. St Paul says, 'Love cannot wrong a neighbour; therefore love is the fulfilment of the law (Rom. 13:10). As we read the psalms, we should think with compassion on the various writers who were struggling with the problem of personal and national misfortune in the face of a caring, powerful God. In the end the problem is not to be solved rationally (by debate or by punishing the wrongdoer). It has to be accepted as a fact of mortal life, and offered to God in prayer. It is then that love enters our heart and a new life opens up for us. This is our introduction to eternity.

Index of Psalms

Psalm numbers are in bold type
Italic page numbers indicate multiple entries

General Index